"TONGUES OF FIRE"

Mary E. Beavers

Copyright © 2005 by Mary Beavers

Tongues of Fire
by Mary Beavers

Printed in the United States of America

ISBN 1-597810-13-4

All rights reserved solely by the author. The author guarantees all contents are original and do not infringe upon the legal rights of any other person or work. No part of this book may be reproduced in any form without the permission of the author. The views expressed in this book are not necessarily those of the publisher.

Unless otherwise indicated, Bible quotations are taken from the King James Version. Copyright © 1996 by Tyndale House Publishers, Inc.

www.xulonpress.com

3/18/06

To Lella & Bill,

May God continue to bless you both!

Mary

TABLE OF CONTENTS

Introduction vii
"Tongues of Fire" 9
"Get Thee Out of Thy Country" 19
"And He Must Needs Go Through Samaria" 27
"Now Then We Are Ambassadors" 37
"These Twelve Jesus Sent Forth" 53
"The Same Commit Thou To Faithful Men" 67
"But the Labourers Are Few" 77
"God Hath Not Given Us A Spirit of Fear" 87
"That These Hands Have Ministered" 97
"As Every Man Hath Received the Gift" 111
Conclusion 117
Notes 119
Bibliography 123
Appendix 125

INTRODUCTION

"Go ye therefore and teach all nations, baptizing them in the name of the Father, and of the Son, and of the Holy Ghost: Teaching them to observe all things whatsoever I have commanded you: and lo, I am with you always, even unto the end of the world." Amen. Matthew 28:19-20

The Great Commission, a mandate which our Lord Jesus Himself received from the Father and gave to His disciples, should still be regarded as the "magna charta" of the Church; for the Lord has made no other plans for the salvation of the lost and the edification of His Kingdom. Jesus' command to the disciples—to *make* disciples of all nations, has never been rescinded; twenty-one centuries later, evangelization of the world remains at the top of God's "To-Do" list, and He's counting on the efforts of *every* believer—and especially those who are in leadership positions in the church—to evangelize within his or her vocation and life-style.

In far too many churches, preachers are satisfied with "evangelizing the evangelized," and the hearers are quite content being "bench warmers" or human sponges—soaking up God's Word, then allowing it to sour, rather than passing it on to impact others' lives. In this twenty-first century, there is a "cry from the desert," and a challenge for the Church to awaken from its complacency—for its members to quit "playing church," and to focus its efforts on a twenty-first century revival of true evangelism—specifically discipleship training and the nurturing of God's people. Too often, a person joins a church, only to "slip through the cracks," either because of a whirl of programs, groups, committees, and services with which they've been bombarded, or because they've simply been *overlooked* or *forgotten about*. Programs, campaigns, fund-raisers, etc., neither teach nor *nurture* people, hence many can be self-destructive to begin with. New converts need the assurance, acceptance, protection, love, support, and fellowship of other believers, for spiritual growth and development. Every believer in Jesus Christ deserves the opportunity of personal nurture and development," says Leroy Eims, in his book, *The Lost Art of Disciple Making.*[1] When Christians are nurtured, they become equipped to *multiply* themselves through ministry.

Besides nurturing disciples, there is a need in God's Church to nurture new converts. Thus, *growing* Christians need continuous nurturing, also, in order that as they mature, they will be equipped to pass on their faith, hence the multiplicative process begins *anew*. One's work is not done until new believers are sharing Jesus with others (Ephesians 4:12-13). The *multiplicative process* (reproducing spiritually qualified workers for Christ) is the only way that Christ's Commission can ever be ultimately carried out. Disciples must be recruited, trained, and nurtured, in order for the multiplication process to take hold. Developing one's full potential of ministry involves the training of other spiritually qualified workers for Christ.

CHAPTER 1

"TONGUES OF FIRE"

> *"And there appeared unto them cloven tongues like as of fire, and it sat upon each of them. And they were all filled with the Holy Ghost, and began to speak with other tongues, as the Spirit gave them utterance." Acts 2:3-4*

John the Baptist had baptized people with water, symbolizing the washing away of their sins, and it coordinated with his message of repentance and reformation; thus, the appearance of the cloven tongues was a fulfillment of his message about the Holy Spirit's baptizing with *fire:* "*I indeed baptize you with water; but one mightier than I cometh, the latchet of whose shoes I am not worthy to unloose: he shall baptize you with the Holy Ghost and with fire*" (Luke 3:16). Within days, this *fire,* of which John was speaking, would manifest itself in *tongues of fire,* heralding the birth of God's Church and the prelude to *evangelism.*

Jesus' baptism with *fire* equipped Him, as well as all who receive Him, with *power* to do God's will. The Holy Ghost signified the *power* needed to do God's will, and Jesus had promised the disciples that they would receive such *power* after they had received the Holy Ghost. But He also let them know that their power was not to be political but spiritual: *"But ye shall receive power, after that the Holy Ghost is come upon you: and ye shall be witnesses unto me, both in Jerusalem, and in all Judea, and in Samaria, and unto the uttermost part of the earth."* (Acts 1:8).

Through *tongues of fire* the disciples would announce to the world that Jesus was indeed the true Messiah, and that His mission was to set the captives free: *"The Spirit of the Lord is upon me, because he hath anointed me to preach the gospel to the poor; he hath sent me to heal the brokenhearted, to preach deliverance to the captives, and recovering of sight to the blind, to set at liberty them that are bruised, to preach the acceptable year of the Lord" (Luke 4:18).*

As the Father took Him back to glory, Jesus went "out of sight," but stayed with His people in a far more real and reaching way, and the power the disciples received, of course went far beyond extraordinary physical strength; it carried with it, **courage**, **boldness**, **confidence**, **insight**, **ability** and *authority*—all of which they would need to obey and fulfill the Great Commission given to them, and to all who call Jesus Savior and Lord (Matthew 28:19-20). On the day of Pentecost (ten days after Jesus' ascension), the Holy Spirit, in the form of *tongues of fire* came upon the believers, empowering them to proclaim Jesus' resurrection in many languages.

The *fire* is a symbol of God's purifying presence—the burning away of the undesirable elements of our lives—setting our hearts aflame to ignite the hearts and lives of others. "Cloven tongues" means the fire separated and rested on each of them. On Mount Sinai, God confirmed the validity of the Old Testament Law with fire from heaven: *"And it came to pass on the third day in the morning, that there were thunders and lightnings, and a thick cloud upon the mount, and the voice of the trumpet exceeding loud; so that all the people that was in the camp trembled"* (Exodus 19:16-18). "At Pentecost, God confirmed the validity of the Holy Spirit's ministry by sending fire. At Mount Sinai, fire came down on one place; at Pentecost, fire came down on many believers, symbolizing that God's presence is now available to all who believe in him."[2]

The Holy Spirit came in the form of *"tongues of fire"* for the proclamation of the Gospel, and could not have come at a more fitting time, for there was a great concourse of people to Jerusalem *from all parts,* for the Feast of Weeks festival. As always, God's timing is perfect and awesome! Also, God's methods and manner are always exact; whereas we read in the Old Testament of God's *coming down* in a cloud (and we know that Christ went up to heaven in a cloud), the Holy Ghost did not descend to earth in a cloud—for His purpose was to "scatter" the clouds that had over spread and cluttered men's minds, blocking them from the Living Truth.

When God wants to affect a change, He is quite capable of making His ministers a *flaming fire: "Who maketh his angels spirits; his ministers a flaming fire"* (Psalm 104:4). Such is evidenced in the testimony of the Prophet Isaiah, who experienced a painful cleansing in order to fulfill the task to which God was calling him. Previously, Isaiah's ministry seemed unsuccessful and he thought of giving it up, but God saw fit to renew his commission—cleansing and purifying him with *fire* sent by one of His seraph. *"Then flew one of the seraphims unto me, having a live coal in his hand, which he had taken with the tongs from off the altar; And he laid it upon my mouth, and said, Lo, this hath touched thy lips; and thine iniquity is taken away, and thy sin purged"* (Isaiah 6:6). Isaiah's new found zeal and *tongue of fire* will be discussed in depth in a later chapter.

The Fire that came down on the day of Pentecost summoned an awakening of the people's senses and expectations, creating *tongues of fire*. Yes, the fire *fell on* them (Acts 2:1-3), the Holy Spirit *came in to* them (v. 4), and the Spirit worked *through* them (v. 41-47). The fire sat upon the disciples to denote the *constant residence* of the Holy Spirit with them, filling them with His many gifts—of which one was the speaking with divers *tongues*.

Though the sign (fire) of the Holy Ghost perhaps disappeared within a short time, the gift of the Spirit would be with them *always*. By the Holy Spirit, and through the disciples, Christ began to speak to the *world*—every man hearing in his own language (Acts 2:6). Filled with the Holy Ghost and more than ever under His sanctifying influences, all one hundred and twenty (Acts 1:15) used their newly given powers and *tongues of fire* for the furtherance of the Gospel, as the Spirit gave them utterance.

Every nationality represented recognized the Gospel in their own language: Galilaeans, Parthians, Medes, Elamites, Cretes, Arabians, Jews, proselytes, and dwellers of Mesopotamia, Judaea, Cappadocia, Pontus, Asia, Phrygia, Pamphylia, Egypt, Libya, Cyrene, and Rome. God offers salvation to all people without regard to nationality, race, color, or language.

By nature, people are unbelieving, and many have a tendency to explain away the miracles of God through *natural* logic; the people witnessing the outpouring of the Holy Spirit on the day of Pentecost were no different. Amazed and perplexed by these *tongues of fire*, some in the crowd accused God's "preachers" of being intoxicated: *"And they were amazed, and were in doubt, saying one to another, What meaneth this? Others mocking said, These men are full of new wine"* (2:12-13). But, man's rationalism has *never* been successful in giving reasonable explanations of anything that is *Divine*, thus Peter had a strong defense against the false charge (Acts 2:15); the birth of the Church was on the horizon!

With his confidence coming from the Holy Spirit, and with the one aim of bringing people to a *saving* knowledge of Jesus Christ, Peter preached his first sermon to a multitude on the streets of Jerusalem. The real power of the Holy Spirit manifest itself, as Peter rose *boldly* to preach his theme: *Jesus is the Messiah, as shown by His resurrection*, and three thousand souls were saved! Peter was making this public proclamation of the resurrection at a time when it could be verified by many witnesses (Many of the people listening were in Jerusalem fifty days earlier at Passover and perhaps had seen or heard about the resurrection of Jesus).

With a *tongue of fire*, Peter capitalized on the tremendous opportunity to share Jesus with such a large audience. He told them who Jesus was and what He had done:

> *"Jesus of Nazareth, a man approved of God among you by miracles and wonders and signs, which God did by him in the midst of you, as ye yourselves also know"* (Acts 2:22).

Peter explains to the people why they should listen to the believers: the Old Testament prophecies had been fulfilled (Joel 2:28-29); because Jesus Christ is the Messiah; and because the *risen* Christ could change their lives eternally.

On his way to preach in the Temple, Peter met a lame man begging at the Beautiful Gate, and accepted the challenge of offering the beggar more than money—the use of his legs and an opportunity to know the God of grace who would restore them! By the authority of Jesus, and willing to use our *tongues of fire,* we too have the power to take people far beyond their immediate source of need. God has such people, waiting with prepared hearts, for our intervention, but we must be totally unselfish to fulfill the call.

If we are willing, and will open our mouths, the Lord will place there the words that He would have His people to hear. At this time, I would like to share a personal testimony:

> On several occasions while traveling, I always had a window seat on an airplane (per my request). I almost prayed each time that the two empty seats beside me would remain unoccupied—so that I would not have to converse with anyone—just simply relax, meditate, or read. In my present walk with the Lord, I can't think of anything more selfish and non-Christlike, on my part. Jesus went *out of His way* to meet unsaved people *where they were.* How many people—how many opportunities did I forsake—for my own comfort and privacy? *"Let brotherly love continue; Be not forgetful to entertain strangers: for thereby some have entertained angels unawares"* (Hebrews 13:1-2). One thing that I desire now, is for God to place people in my path that I can witness to—never to withhold my *"tongue of fire"* again!

Just as there were many witnesses to verify Peter's proclamation, as believers, we have the Word of God as our witness, and we have His Spirit dwelling within us. So, where are the *tongues of fire* today? If God should ask, "Whom shall I send, and who will go for us," as a Church, how will we answer? Will we say, as did Isaiah, *"Here am I, Lord, send me?"* Or will we be like Jonah, and think, "Here am I, Lord, send somebody else?" *Tongues of fire* are not just reserved for preachers, teachers, and evangelists, but to every believer who has asked Jesus Christ to come into their lives, and has said, "yes" to His will and to His way.

With a world so in need, the Christian community cannot afford to sit back and hope that the full time ministers and evangelists of God's Word will accomplish the mission *alone.* The fulfilment of the Great Commission to "Go into all the world and preach the Gospel to every creature" is the *shared* responsibility of every believer, and we must take initiative—whether quietly or openly. We must live as salt and light—Christ's agents of healing a broken world. Our mission is to make visible the invisible God to an unbelieving world, and to do so in many instances will entail the crossing of traditional boundaries and barriers—through contact and association.

We must become redemptive neighbors, co-workers, friends, and relatives. We are called to love (John 13:34), serve (Galatians 5:13), identify need (Acts 4:34-35) and respond (Romans 4:13) to all people, not just fellow believers. "Outsiders to faith are first drawn to Christians and then to Christ. Unfortunately, not all Christians attract. Like a turned magnet, some repel. Yet Christians, alive to God, loving, caring, laughing, sharing, involved at the point of people's need, present an undeniable witness for Christ in their society."[3]

With the same *"tongues of fire"* that birthed the early church, how many souls can we reach in our churches, on the streets, at crusades or revivals today? "This same Jesus," by way of the same Enabler and Comforter, stands ready to empower today's Church and its people, to affect the same glorious teaching, fellowship, signs and wonders, and above all, *salvation* that took place in the early Church. After Peter's powerful, Spirit-filled message on the day of Pentecost, the people were deeply moved, and wanted to know,

"What shall we do?" This is the same question that the people of today must ask, and prepared people are needed—everywhere, to lead them to Christ.

But being led to Christ and being forgiven is only the first step for the new convert; they need to know that: 1) they must strive to live like forgiven people; 2) they are now a part of the Great Commission themselves, and must therefore exercise their *tongues of fire* whenever and wherever the Lord provides the opportunity; 3) they are expected to be a part of the multiplication process—to make disciples themselves.

Even in areas of the world whereby people cannot read, there are strategic evangelism ministries in place. One is a world-class team of eight Chronological Bible Storying (CBS) specialists, led by Dr. Avery T. Willis, Jr. The movement is designed to disciple the 70% of the world's unreached who are "Oral Learners," and are effectively communicating God's Word to them. Because of these *tongues of fire*, the Gospel is getting to unreached people groups and non-literates—teaching them to *make disciples*, leaders are becoming better equipped, and churches are being planted. Pre-literates, functionally illiterates, semi-literates, storying cultures and many others who simply prefer a non-literate approach, can now be evangelized, discipled and prepared for leadership.[4]

Indeed, God has not changed His plan of evangelizing the world, and we can clearly grasp this truth in a legend that recounts the return of Jesus to glory after His time on earth:

> Even in heaven he bore the marks of His earthly pilgrimage with its cruel cross and shameful death. The angel Gabriel approached Him and said, "Master, you must have suffered terribly for men down there." *"I did,"* He said. "And, continued Gabriel, "do they know all about how you loved them and what you did for them?" *"Oh no,"* Jesus said, *"not yet. Right now only a handful of people in Palestine know."* Gabriel was perplexed. "Then what have you done," he asked "to let everyone know about your love for them?" Jesus said, *"I've asked Peter, James, John, and a few more friends to tell other people about Me. Those who are told will in turn tell still other people about Me, and My story will be spread* to the farthest reaches of the globe.

Ultimately, all of mankind will have heard about My life and what I have done." Gabriel frowned and looked rather skeptical. He knew well what poor stuff men were made of. "Yes, he said, "but what if Peter, James, and John grow weary? What if the people who come after them forget? What if way down in the twentieth century, people just don't tell others about you? Haven't you made any other plans?" And Jesus answered, *"I haven't made any other plans. I'm counting on them."*

God sent a *Tongue of fire* into the world to unveil the "great mystery" of the Kingdom of God (Mark 4:11) that offers salvation to mankind, and He is not willing that *any* should perish: *The Lord is not slack concerning his promise, as some men count slackness; but is longsuffering to us-ward, not willing that any should perish, but that all should come to repentance"* (2 Peter 3:9). There is a *"tongue of fire"* in every believer, not intended to be the raging, destructive fire (James 3:6) with irreversible damage, but rather, one that is controlled with the help of the Holy Spirit, who will give us increasing power to monitor what we say. Our *tongues of fire* are to be used in the presence and power of the Holy Spirit to proclaim the Good News of Jesus Christ.

John the Baptist prepared the way for the Lamb of God, and people that do not know the Lamb need to be *prepared* to meet Him. But how can they get to know Him without *tongues of fire?* With these *tongues of fire* we can prepare others by explaining their need for forgiveness, and telling them how Christ can give their lives meaning. John the Baptist used his *tongue of fire* to share his faith, and as a result, attracted many people. People today are equally in need of words that have meaning for their lives—words that not only tell them of a Savior's blood that can wash away all their sins, but also a love that can embrace them forever and live with Him in a land that will never grow old.

When compared to the apostles, we as believers naturally tend to think of ourselves as being ineffective, and indeed, there are some forces, obstacles and influences that may hinder our effectiveness. Evangelism may not be every Christian's gift, but God has made it crystal clear in His Word that every Christian is to *"go"* and make disciples of all nations, and then teach these new disciples how to, in turn, make disciples (multiply themselves).

The proceeding chapters of this writing will attempt to help others to understand the true meaning of evangelism and discipleship, give some how-to's of sharing Christ with others—in order that *tongues of fire* may once again be heard from our churches, work places, schools, homes, and social institutions.

CHAPTER 2

"GET THEE OUT OF THY COUNTRY"

"Now the Lord had said unto Abram, Get thee out of thy country, and from thy kindred, and from thy father's house, unto a land that I will show thee: And I will make of thee a great nation...... and in thee shall all families of the earth be blessed. So Abram departed." Genesis 12:1-4

The Birth of Evangelism

From the onset of creation, God's desire was to have a people set apart for the purpose of having a relationship with Him and worshiping Him. *"Let them praise the name of the Lord: for he commanded, and they were created. He hath also stablished them for ever and ever: he hath made a decree which shall not pass"* (Psalm 148:5-6). God created mankind in His own image (Genesis 1:26), but those with whom God would enjoy eternal communion—Adam and Eve, shattered His hopes by willfully disobeying Him and breaking fellowship with their Creator and Sustainer (3:6-19).

From the first "bite" of the forbidden fruit, God's grace

fashioned the blessing of *Salvation*, and Jesus started walking towards Calvary (3:15). A way of spreading His *Good News* would soon be manifested. Henceforth from the Fall, and the repopulation of the earth through Noah (Genesis, chapters 9 and 10), two distinct groups of people have existed: those who show indifference to sin and evil, and those who "call upon the name of the Lord" (4:26). The latter group would have the awesome responsibility of being ambassadors with the *Good News*—the Old Testament *"tongues of fire!"* Evangelism was indeed on the horizon. Although only a handful of people really tried to follow God, He was still determined to develop a nation of people that He could call His own—a *remnant* of people—who for forty-two generations, would keep the flame of *evangelism* burning until the advent of the Messiah. God would establish His nation of people by calling a man from a heathen country—Ur of the Chaldees—by anointing a man named Abram as His first *evangelist*.

The command which God gave to Abram flows right along with the *Gospel call*—the Great Commission (Matthew 28:19-20), and since we are all called to be ambassadors for Christ, we must do the same as Abram—we must forsake natural affections and give way to Divine grace. While our family, friends, and associates may be a constant temptation to us, we may at times have to also forsake them, lest we be infected by them. We may be tried whether we love God better than all: *"If any man come to me, and hate not his father, and mother, and wife, and children, and brethren, and sisters, yea, and his own life also, he cannot be my disciple"* (Luke 14:26).

God may choose to send any one of us to an unknown place, with a "to be announced" agenda, for the proclamation of His Word. He took Abram from his own people—fellow idolaters, and promised to make him the head of another people in another land: *"In thee shall all the families of the earth be blessed"* (12:3). No doubt, both friends and relatives had their various reactions to Abram's obedience to this God of the Hebrews—most of which were probably negative. After all, Abram was not a young man apt for adventure and exploration of his options; he was seventy-five years old (v.4).

As we see in this covetous, greed-driven, self-serving world which we live, the norm is not to come out of one's "comfort zone," to accommodate the needs of others. It is a "I've got mine–you get yours" world. But tempted as he might have been to stay and mingle with his kindred—when God said, "Get thee out of thy country and from thy kindred," Abram got out, trusting God to make up for all he could lose or leave behind. Each person must ask himself or herself, "Can I leave *all* to go with God?" Remember, the call to "go" is not an option—it is a *command*!

Abram set a precedent for other faithful servants of God, who answered the call to evangelism—to preserve a *remnant* of people for God. Prior to God's calling of Abram, Noah, a uniquely righteous man of 480 years, was given a colossal and almost impossible task. He was told to "go" and build an ark, to save God's remnant from the destruction of a flood: *"And God said unto Noah, The end of all flesh is come before me; for the earth is filled with violence through them...I will destroy them...Make thee an ark....I do bring a flood of waters upon the earth..."* (Genesis 6:13-17).

No one had ever even heard of rain before, for God had always caused a mist to come up from the earth to water the whole face of the ground (Genesis 2:5-6). The flood didn't come until Noah's 600th year, and in the interim, he had to serve as a "preacher of righteousness," a *tongue of fire* to a wayward people. Noah was perhaps the recipient of much ridicule and rebellion from the godless, but remained faithful and obedient to God. *"And Noah did according unto all that the Lord commanded him"* (Genesis 6:22; 7:7:5). Noah stuck to his project, no matter what!

Many of us have difficulty sticking to any project, whether or not it is directed by God. One reason may be that as humans, we look for immediate "micro-wave" results. But in the case of evangelism—following God's command to "go," we must trust God. And the only way to trust Him is to know Him. The only way to know Him, of course is to stay in communion with Him, through prayer, and the study of His Word. In spite of the sin, evil, and corruption surrounding our lives, we would do well to follow Noah's example of obedience and wholehearted love for God.

God can request anything of us, because He *is* God. But one thing we know for certain—He will always supply what is needed: *"But my God shall supply all your need according to his riches in glory"* (Phillipians 4:19); and He will neither leave us, nor forsake us (Hebrews 13:5). We, too can be living examples in our generation—walking step by step in faith with God. Obedience is a long term commitment, but God is always faithful to those who obey Him and strive for righteous living. Thus, Noah was honored by God with an everlasting covenant that would benefit all future generations: *"And I, behold, I establish my covenant with you, and with your see after you....neither shall all flesh be cut off any more by the waters of a flood; neither shall there any more be a flood to destroy the earth. I do set my bow in the cloud...."* (Genesis 9:12-17).

From the birth of Genesis to the end of the prophecy of Malachi, Scripture is full of faithful, committed saints who carried the torch of evangelism, in order for God to complete His purpose for mankind. But from that time to the birth of Jesus Christ, there were four hundred years of blackness—four hundred years of stillness without any prophetic voice. God chose not to speak to His people, but when He did, it was through the "burning and shining light" of John the Baptist." *"He was a burning and shining light:*

and ye were willing for a season to rejoice in his light" (John 5:35).

For four hundred and fifty years, one hundred and twenty priests and elders ruled over Israel. Then suddenly, unexpectedly, and certainly dramatically, a strange man appears in the wilderness—a loner, to speak to a non-Jewish audience. *"In those days came John the Baptist, preaching in the wilderness of Judaea, and saying, Repent ye for the kingdom of heaven is at hand"* (Matthew 3:1-2). This wild-looking man of remarkable character had no power or position in the Jewish political system, but he spoke the *truth* with almost irresistible *authority*—moving hundreds to repentance but some also to resistance and resentment, with his *tongue of fire*.

John had his work cut out for him, as the people he preached to came from everywhere—North, South, East and West, and from all levels of society. What he said about their character speaks volumes: *"But when he saw many of the Pharisees and Sadducees come to his baptism, he said unto them, O generation of vipers, who hath warned you to flee from the wrath to come?"* (v. 7). With a *tongue of fire*, John criticized and challenged this legalistic and hypocritical group. The political and religious pulse of Jerusalem was not the best with which to work.

Paul Ravenhill, in one of his sermons described it as such: "John the Baptist appears in the wilderness. It was not only a wilderness geographically, it was a wilderness morally, it was a wilderness politically, it was a wilderness religiously."[5] But in spite of the political and religious chaos, John was a fearless, uncompromising confronter—this "desert preacher" had both the *Truth* as well as the *authority* of God, working for him. When you are thus equipped, even a corrupt, hard hearted man like Herod can be moved to admit his sin (Mark 6:26).

Though Herod got rid of the "desert preacher" (honoring

the request of his illegal wife), he was not able to stop John's message or his mission. The One John had announced was already on *His* mission! *"Now when Jesus had heard that John was cast into prison, he departed into Galilee...From that time Jesus began to preach, and to say, Repent: for the kingdom of heaven is at hand"* (Matthew 4:12-17).

God doesn't guarantee an easy life to any of us who serve Him, but being used of Him was all that mattered to John, which made him uncompromising in his confrontation of the unsaved. With a *tongue of fire*, John was preaching repentance, preparing the Way—the same Way that you and I are *to proclaim*—Jesus! Like John, we, too must be determined not to sacrifice, compromise, or jeopardize the *Truth* when we witness to unbelievers. Both our witness and our testimony can be strong tools in our evangelistic message; thus, they must be clear and forceful. And, there is no witness without a testimony: One's experience of God's faithfulness is the substance of his or her testimony.

Three things we can use from John the Baptist's short ministry: 1) We are not guaranteed an easy or safe life while serving God, for our message will not be any more popular than that of John. 2) Standing for the *Truth* is more important than life itself. 3) The greatest investment in life is doing what God desires of us.

Before any of our previous "evangelists" were told to "go," God had reached into eternity and sent the *Truth*, who would eventually tell us all to "go." Jesus was willing to "go," all the way from eternity back to eternity, to give us the gift of Salvation—to be offered to all who would believe: *"For God so loved the world, that He gave His only begotten So; that whosoever believeth in Him shall not perish, but have everlasting life"* (John 3:16).

Before telling us to "go," Jesus, our Savior and Lord asked God to first sanctify us. *"Sanctify them through thy truth: thy word is thy truth. As thou hast sent me into the world, even so have I also sent them into the world"* (John 17:18). Jesus credited us as being "not of the world," (v. 16) but in it. And He didn't ask God to take us "out" of the world, rather, to use us *in* the world. Knowing that Jesus prayed for our protection (v. 15), should give us the confidence that we need to evangelize in the world. Jesus is our perfect Model for evangelism.

CHAPTER 3

"AND HE MUST NEEDS GO THROUGH SAMARIA"

God's vision of a church includes all people (Jews and Gentiles) united in their love for Him. Regardless of race, color, creed, social standing, or past sins, the Gospel of Jesus Christ (Salvation) is for every person: *"For I am not ashamed of the gospel of Christ: for it is the power of God unto salvation to every one that believeth; to the Jew first, and also to the Greek. For therein is the righteousness of God revealed from faith to faith"* (Romans 1:16-17). Persons are saved through faith in Christ, not because they are a part of a particular nation, religion, or family—a truth rejected by the "pure" Jews. Jesus is our perfect Role Model in evangelism, for He crossed *all* barriers to share the Gospel; we must thus be willing to penetrate *cultural, religious,* and *social barriers* to share the Good News at any time in any place.

There was deep hatred between Jews and Samaritans (a mixed race produced through intermarriage between foreigners and the Jews from the Northern Kingdom). The Jews saw themselves as *pure* descendants of Abraham, and their hatred for this "impure" race was so strong that they traveled a longer route *around* the city of Samaria, subjecting themselves to attacks by robbers and murderers (Luke 10:30). Concerning the Samaritans' regard for Jesus, they would not receive Him and His followers in their village when He was in route to Jerusalem: *"And they would not receive him, because his face was as though he would go to Jerusalem"* (Luke 9:53).

Why should Jesus even care that these people hear the Gospel? Even James and John, when rejected by the Samaritans, wanted to retaliate by commanding fire to come down from heaven to consume them (v. 54). But Jesus rebuked them by saying, *"Ye know not what manner of spirit ye are of. For the Son of man is not come to destroy men's lives, but to save them"* (v.55). To save them! To save people who have rejected you! But it is this kind of resolve that should characterize the Christian's life also.

It is a human reaction (and Jesus was all human as well as all Divine) to retaliate—to "get even" with those who mistreat us or deny us. Forgiving is simply not the norm, even for Christians. Even if we resolve to forgive, we can't *forget*. Why? Because we only focus on our immediate circumstances, rather than the long range purpose of the Kingdom; we just cannot stand to be "dumped on." Yet, when God gives us a course of action—such as the Great Commission, we are expected to move steadily toward our destination, regardless of any potential hazards. Jesus knew that he was facing persecution and death in Jerusalem, but still, "He must needs" go there.

Jesus has demonstrated, hundreds of times in Scripture, that we must focus on the *lost sheep of the house of Israel—* that is why He is our perfect Role Model in evangelism. Like the Jews, Jesus could have taken a different route to Galilee, but He had some "fishing" to do, and He would dangle His "bait" in the presence of a *Samaritan woman* with whom He would engage in one of the greatest discourses of His ministry; a discourse that gave a woman a *tongue of fire* that changed the world—thus, creating *tongues of fire* that would send a man to the desert to proclaim the Gospel (the Ethiopian eunuch). It would send another who would be willing to accept martyrdom for Kingdom building (Stephen); yet, another who would go from persecutor to "Apostle to the Gentiles" (Paul).

Previously, Jesus had preached to multitudes, but now He condescends to teach a single person, which is a lesson, not just for evangelists, but for ministers as well—save but one soul from death! Jesus' subject is a woman— a poor woman; she's a stranger, and she's a Samaritan—but it would be through this vessel that Jesus would sow the seed of the Gospel in Samaria. He would forsake his weariness and hunger (John 4:6-8) for this opportunity to save *many* souls through her. Just as Jesus crossed all sorts of barriers to offer Living Water to this woman, we who follow Him must be prepared to do the same.

Although she had never had any opportunity of seeing Christ's miracles, the Samaritan woman was prepared to receive Jesus in her heart. "God can make the light of grace shine *into the heart* even where He doth not make the light of the Gospel shine *in the face*."[6] God has *prepared hearts* waiting, and as Christians, *our hearts* should be beating for these people. But our hearts must first beat with the Master's heart, which beats for all who are separated from Him.

God has empowered us to witness, and has given each of us an experience with Jesus to *share*. He will use the life and words of every Christian to reach the unbeliever. Each of us are on assignment from our Lord to reach the lost— God has arranged divine appointments for us to share Jesus often and in all kinds of places, and with all kinds of people. He has empowered us, and our hearts should be beating with His heart. Like Jesus, we must look for open doors and be sensitive to the people we meet.

Jesus has taught us not to escape from the world or avoid all relationships with non-Christians; but to come out of our "comfort zones" for the sake of His Kingdom. He has also taught us how to be salt and light (Matthew 5:13-16), and how to have intimacy with and compassion for people. Jesus not only went through Samaria to save a wretched woman—He touched a leper, healed a woman who wasn't even suppose to touch Him (Luke 8:44), and ate with sinners, all because God desires *back* the souls of all who are willing. We, too, should be able now to see beyond the myriad of layers of people, and know what they truly long for or need—peace in the Lord. We must not allow anything to extinguish our *tongue of fire*.

Tongues of fire were to reach the *uttermost parts of the world* (Acts 1:8), and the continent of Africa was no exception. In the middle of his exciting and successful preaching ministry to great crowds in Samaria (Acts 8:58), God directed Philip (the deacon) to "go" to the desert for an appointment with an Ethiopian eunuch. To some, it would have been a demotion, but to Philip it was an opportunity to be one of the first to obey Jesus' command to *go*—to take the Gospel to the "uttermost parts of the world."

Because Philip was willing to obey his Master wholeheartedly, an opportunity opened up for the introduction of Christianity to a heathen country (vv.26-39). There was a cry from the desert! Here we have an example of one who is not so renowned as Paul, nor divine in nature and power as Jesus, to illustrate God's use of *anyone* who is *willing* to follow Him. God opens doors of opportunity to His ministers and lay people in some of the most unlikely places. Here, it is a desert—a place Philip would never have thought of working!

There was a small probability of even finding work in the desert. Hence, none of Jesus' other followers had appeared anxious to leave Jerusalem. In face, it had taken intense persecution to scatter the believers from Jerusalem to Judea and Samaria where God had instructed them to go. Due to the age-old prejudice, Samaria was the last place many of the Jews would go; but Philip had gone there, and many Samaritans responded in large numbers. Now he was in the desert, with his *tongue of fire*, ready to preach Jesus!

This Ethiopian man had been in Jerusalem for worship, and was returning and sitting in his chariot reading the prophet Isaiah (8:28) when the Spirit said to Philip: *"Go near, and join thyself to this chariot"* (v. 29). Talk about the providence and grace of God!

And a willing servant of God, with a willing heart! Philip didn't even have to throw his line in the water for this *catch*! All he had to do was be *available to God*, and willing to "go!" Philip also was not shy to strangers, nor affected by this man's position.

The eunuch was a man of *great position and authority* in his own country. He wasn't *driving* the chariot—he was *riding in it*, and had charge of all Queen Candace's treasure; "all the queen's money! *"Behold, a man of Ethiopia, an eunuch of great authority under Candace queen of the Ethiopians, who had the charge of all her treasure, and had come to Jerusalem to worship"* (v. 27).

A question for us as Christians is "How are we with strangers that we meet on the road—do we avoid them, as I once did (Chapter 1), or do we ask for the Spirit's help in discerning our move?" Philip may not have known all that God would have him to do in the desert, but one thing is certain—he knew that this was a *divine* appointment. As Christians, we also need to walk in lock-step with God, *trusting* his lead all the way! Philip doesn't walk up to the chariot—he *runs* to the man, and is anxious to get a conversation going, because it's evangelism time!

The providence of God has placed this man—a man of a

different country, culture, and race, in the path of one who would drop everything and "go," in order that one more lost "lamb" could be found. And Philip does just that—he opens the dialogue by showing interest in what the man was reading: *"Understandest thou what thou readest?"* Philip obviously had been diligent in searching the Scriptures and was thus prepared to explain them to the man.

We must study what the Word of God says so that we can *understand* what it means: *"Study to shew thyself approved unto God, a workman that needeth not to ashamed, rightly dividing the word of truth"* (2 Timothy 2:15). We must build our lives on God's Word, as well as build His Word into our lives. God's Word is *"profitable for doctrine, for reproof, for correction, for instruction in righteousness: that the man of God may be perfect, thoroughly furnished unto all good works"* (2 Timothy 3:16-17). God's Word also tells us how to live for Him, and how to serve Him and others.

We can learn much from the eunuch by studying his answer to Philip's question: *"How can I, except some man should guide me"* (v. 31). Like this man, we should: a) never let pride or insecurity get in the way of understanding God's Word; b) we should always be desirous to be taught. Not one of us will ever know everything. If we were to read the Bible fifty times, still we would never know everything, for each time we read it, something that we have never seen before will be revealed to us. The reason is that the more we seek God, the more He will *reveal* to us: *"For he that cometh to God must believe that he is, and that he is a rewarder of them that diligently seek him"* (Hebrews 11:6).

The Scripture that was unclear to the Ethiopian was: *"He was led as a sheep to the slaughter; and like a lamb dumb before his shearer, so opened he not his mouth....for his life is taken from the earth"* (Isaiah 53:7-8). The eunuch wanted to know who the prophet Isaiah was referring to—

himself, or another man? Immediately, Philip did what we all have been commanded to do—he PREACHED JESUS! What does it mean to preach Jesus? It means to preach His birth, life, death, burial and resurrection!

But I can only imagine that Philip, with a *tongue of fire*, took the Ethiopian on an "Emmaus" type walk, beginning with the promised Seed in Genesis chapters 3 and 12, moving on to the prophecies. The next stop would be the synoptic Gospels (Matthew, Mark, Luke) to recapture Jesus' birth, life, crucifixion, and resurrection, then back to the *beginning* in John 1—where the Word became flesh and dwelt among us. Philip's effectiveness in sharing the Gospel with the Ethiopian eunuch brought Christianity into the power structures of another country and government (Ethiopia) as well as another continent, Africa. *Tongues of fire* were gaining ground!

The next great evangelist we will study, unlike the others, was not asked to leave his comfort zone, rather, he was literally "knocked out" of his comfort zone. Saul, the greatest persecutor of Christ and Christians was traveling to Damascus to track down yet more Christians when he was confronted by the risen Christ, who brought him face-to-face with the Truth of the Gospel: *"And as he journeyed, he came near Damascus: and suddenly there shined round about him* a light from heaven: *and he fell to the earth, and heard, and heard a voice saying unto him, Saul, Saul, why persecutest thou me? And he said who art thou, Lord? And the Lord said, I am Jesus whom thou persecutest: it is hard for thee to kick against the pricks"* (Acts 9:3-5). For Saul, it was time to *go*!

Whereas Saul thought that he was persecuting heretics, the Lord let him know that in truth, he was persecuting Him, and in turn, was only hurting himself. Even today, anyone who persecutes believers is guilty of persecuting Jesus (Matthew 25:40, 45), because believers *are* the Body of

Christ on earth: *"And the King shall answer and say unto them, Verily I say unto you, Inasmuch as ye did it not unto one of the least of these my brethren, ye did it not to me"* (Matthew 25:45). Little did Saul know that God was readying him to "go," to help His Church, and to preach the risen Christ throughout the Roman Empire, on three missionary journeys.

Out of his "comfort zone," and with a new name (Paul), this former persecutor of Jews, became the Apostle to the Gentiles—fighting for them against thorny issues of law, and particularly *circumcision*. Paul worked tediously to convince the Jews that the Gentiles were acceptable to God, and even harder to convince the Gentiles that they were worthy of God's love and free gift of Salvation. Paul stood against the Judaizers, who accused him of watering down the Gospel to make it easier for Gentiles to accept, and opposed Peter on the issue of circumcision being a requirement for Gentile Salvation.

Paul's epistles comprise most of the New Testament, but his testimony in Philippians best speaks of the transformation of his life: *"For me to live is Christ, and to die is gain"* (1:21). Paul's actual works in evangelism will be covered in depth in the chapters on *discipleship*.

God sometimes uses both change and pain in accomplishing His purpose, and as His *vessels,* we never know where our *"must need*s" will take us. For Jesus, it was Samaria, where a woman—culturally and morally "unfit" could be empowered to say, *come see a man"* (John 4:29), bringing many Samaritans into the *fold.* For Philip, it was to the desert, to plant the seed of evangelism in Africa. For Saul, it was the Damascus road, a road that would take the Gospel first to the Jews and then to the Gentiles. Each of us would do well to ask ourselves, "where will my 'must needs' take me? Better yet, what will be my response?"

We all live in the midst of hurting people who desperately

need to know Jesus Christ as Savior and Lord, and they are in various places: the marketplace (employer, fellow workers), friends, business contacts, school, family, and even *church*. As Christians, we have a tendency to sit and worship in "our own" little pews, only reaching out if the pastor initiates a "greeting time." But many of the people that we worship with on Sunday are lonely, isolated, discouraged, defeated people. We cannot afford to assume that "all is well with them" and go on our merry way.

We can't even assume that all who are in church are believers. This is a "WWJD" (What would Jesus do?) time. Jesus was never so wrapped up in His divinity that He couldn't extend Himself to people. He met them where they were and spent time with them, even attending their social gatherings (Luke 7:34). Are we willing to extend ourselves to those not in our own circle, to respond to our own "must needs?"

CHAPTER 4

"NOW THEN WE ARE AMBASSADORS"

It is said that there are as many definitions of evangelism as there are evangelists, thirty-one different ones being cited in one chapter of the Tambaram Series by John Mott in 1939,[7] hence, scholars, theologians, missionary councils, journalists, and even evangelists themselves have pondered and debated over the guidelines for establishing a wholistic *definition* of evangelism. In each approach to defining evangelism, these men and women have fervently argued over semantics, dynamism, energy, intentionality, Christology, etc. To quote a few definitions of evangelism:

In 1918, the Anglican definition for evangelism read as such: "To evangelize is to present Christ Jesus in the power of the Holy Spirit, that men shall come to put their trust in God through Him, to accept Him as their Saviour, and serve Him as their King in the fellowship of His Church."[8] Another widely quoted definition of evangelism is that of D.T. Nile's in 1951: "It is one beggar telling another beggar where to get food."[9] Niles goes on to explain that the Christian does not offer out of his own bounty, because he has no bounty; rather, he is simply a guest at his Master's table and, as evangelist, he calls others too.

The Lausanne Covenant Definition, drawn up by the International Congress on World Evangelization in Switzerland in July of 1974 defines evangelism in these words: "To evangelize is to spread the good news that Jesus Christ died for our sins and was raised from the dead according to the Scriptures, and that as the reigning Lord he now offers the forgiveness of sins and the liberating gift of the Spirit to all who repent and believe."[10]

A Church Growth Definition of evangelism, developed by Donald McGavran and Winfield Arn speaks of evangelism as: "To proclaim Jesus Christ as God and Savior, to persuade people to become his disciples and responsible members of his church."[11]

Writer George Hunter, who taught at the Perkins School of Theology of Southern Methodist University in Dallas Texas gave us three definitions of evangelism: "Evangelism is what WE do to help make the Christian faith, life, and mission a live option to undiscipled people, both outside and inside the congregation; evangelism is also what JESUS CHRIST does through the church's *kerygma* (message), *koinonia* (fellowship), and *diakonia* (service) to set people free; evangelism happens when the RECEIVER turns to Christ, to the Christian message and ethic, to a Christian congregation, and to the world, in love and mission—*in any order.*"[12]

Last, but certainly not least, Delos Miles, Southern Baptist Practitioner and theoretician of evangelism believes that evangelism is ecumenical and eclectic, both in its methodology and its theology—and spent two decades working on the following definition of evangelism: *Evangelism is being, doing, and telling the Gospel of the kingdom of God, in order that by the power of the Holy Spirit persons and structures may be converted to the lordship of*

Jesus Christ. "this is my present definition of evangelism. It has been in process for nearly two decades. And while I am not completely satisfied with it, I am willing to live by it and to defend it."[13]

Each phrase in Mile's definition is scripturally supported of it, as evangelism is explicitly tied to the Gospel, for it is the Good News that God sent Jesus Christ into the world to redeem it. *"But when the fullness of time was come, God sent forth his Son, made of a woman, made under the law. To redeem them that were under the law, that we might receive the adoption of sons"* (Galatians 4:4, 5). Because of the attention given to both the theoretical as well as the practical aspects of evangelism, I have been led, by the Spirit, to closely examine the definition supported by Miles.

In examining Mile's definition of evangelism, four words or phrases stand out distinctively:

Gospel
Kingdom of God Enterprise
Holy Spirit
Converted.

Gospel:

The **Gospel**—the Good News about Jesus Christ is at the heart of our evangelistic message, and it is *good news!* The Gospel is good news for all persons and for every person everywhere: it is good news for the poor as well as the rich; good news for the intellectual as well as the illiterate; good news for the blind; good news for the prisoner; good news for the "master" as well as the "slave." The Gospel is for every race, color, and creed: *"For there is no difference between the Jew and the Greek: for the same Lord over all is rich unto all that call upon him. For whosoever shall call upon the name of the Lord shall be saved"*

(Romans 10:12-13).

The **Gospel**—the *Jesus* Story that can raise from the dead those who are dead in their trespasses and sins: *"Likewise reckon ye also yourselves to be dead indeed to sin, but alive unto God through Jesus Christ our Lord"* (Romans 6:11). When we unite and identify with Christ, our old sinful nature is to be regarded as *dead* and unresponsive to sin. We should no longer pursue our old agendas, desires, and goals, because we have a new life; thus, the Holy Spirit—the Comforter that Jesus left with us, will enable us to become all that Christ wants us to be.

The **Gospel**—the *Christ* Story, can actually be said to be Christ Himself. The Word itself became flesh (John 1:14), it became human. God became a man—not part man and part God—but completely human and *still* completely *divine!* *"For in him dwelleth all the fulness of the Godhead bodily"* (Colossians 2:9). In asserting Christ's deity, Paul stressed that in Christ there is all of God in a human body. So, the **Gospel** is the good news that God was in Christ, reconciling the world unto Himself, and the keys that Jesus spoke of in Matthew 16:19 are the **Gospel** by which the gates of heaven are to be opened or kept shut. "Our binding or loosing the **Gospel** determines to a great extent who is saved and who is lost. What an awesome thought!"[14]

Kingdom of God Enterprise:

That evangelism is a **Kingdom-of-God** enterprise—the enterprise of wrestling enemy occupied territory (earth) and restoring it to its rightful Owner can be seen in the activity of the early Christian messengers, who certainly *"turned the world upside down"* (Acts 17:6) These Christians revolutionized lives, crossed all social and cultural barriers, caused people to *care deeply* for one another, and stirred them to worship their God! With a Kingdom of God mind-set, they were more about dynamically transforming lives than they were about promoting *programs* in the Church.

Man has had a blueprint from day six of creation, for God has provided the perfect blueprint for man to follow in developing a **Kingdom-of-God enterprise**. Whereas He has ultimate authority and dominion over the earth, God has chosen to delegate *some* of it to the human race, a blessing—second only to being created in His image (Genesis 1:26). So, His original plan, of course, was for man to have dominion over the earth (1:28). To have dominion over something (according to Webster's Dictionary) is to have the *power to rule—absolute authority and control* over it—always willing to do battle with the enemy, Satan.

Having dominion over the earth includes not only readying ourselves for battle with the enemy (Ephesians 6:18), but also our mission in this world—our service to *unbelievers*—continuing what Jesus started. Jesus calls us not only to come to Him (Matthew 11:28), but also to *go* for Him. "Your mission is so significant that Jesus repeated it five times, in five different ways, in five different books of the Bible. It is as if He was saying, "I really want you to get this!"[15] In this **Kingdom of God Enterprise**, we are working with God and representing Him; in other words, we get to *partner with God* in the building of His Kingdom. Oh, to be so blessed!

Holy Spirit:

That evangelism is dependent upon the power of the **Holy Spirit** can be validated by the fact it is *He*—and *only He* who opens doors for evangelization; so He is the Chief Dynamic of evangelism. The early Church did not start or grow by its own power or enthusiasms. The disciples were *empowered* by God's Spirit—the promised Comforter and Guide sent when Jesus ascended to heaven: "But ye shall receive power, after that the Holy Ghost is come upon you: and ye shall be witnesses unto me both in Jerusalem, and in all Judaea, and in Samaria, and unto the uttermost part of the earth (Acts 1:8). And, by faith, all believers can claim the **Holy Spirit's** power to do the work of God.

Paul testified of the **Holy Spirit's** impact upon his ministry in Romans 15:19: *"Through mighty signs and wonders, by the power of the Spirit of God.....I have fully preached the gospel of Christ"* (Romans 15:19). As any Christian should, Paul studied and prepared for his ministry, but his confidence came from knowing that the **Holy Spirit** was helping and guiding his words: *"And my speech and my preaching was not with enticing words of man's wisdom, but in demonstration of the Spirit and of power: that your faith should not stand in the wisdom of men, but in the power of God"* (1 Corinthians 2:4).

When the apostles met furious opposition in the days of the early church (including arrests), the **Holy Spirit** opened the prison doors and brought them forth to continue their evangelism: *"But the angel of the Lord by night opened the prison doors, and brought them forth"* (Acts 5:19). He also opened the door of the continents of Africa (Acts 8), and Europe (13:2; 16:6).

Thus, this Third Person of the Trinity is still opening doors today—all over the world—including China, where the Church of Jesus Christ is said to be growing at an unprecedented rate! The reason? An ever-increasing number of lay people are responding to the prompting of the **Holy Spirit** to realize their privilege and responsibility to *"go!"*

Converted:

According to Miles, the intention of evangelism is to **convert** persons and structures to the lordship of Jesus Christ. "Structures" include the *family (*nuclear, extended, tribe, caste, clan, and all ethnic groupings of humanity), and the Church. Miles sees the evangelist as a *change* agent, dealing first and foremost with that change called *repentance.* "The most profound change any person can ever experience is biblical repentance.

Conversion is a fundamental change in persons—a cleansing from the inside out."[16] We know that evangelism seeks to make new persons: *"Therefore If any man be in Christ he is a new creature*: old things are passed away; behold, all things become new"* (2 Corinthians 5:17).

The Holy Spirit helps us to become brand-new people on the inside, giving us new life; we are not reformed, rehabilitated, or educated—we are *new* creations, living in vital union with our Savior and Lord, Jesus Christ. We are not merely turning over a new leaf in life, rather, we are *beginning* a new life under a *new Master*! *"As ye have therefore received Christ Jesus the Lord, so walk ye in him: rooted and built up in him, and stablished in the faith, as ye have been taught, abounding therein with thanksgiving"* (Colossians 2:6).

Jesus is our Root (Revelation 5:5), and we are to draw our life-giving strength from Him, just as plants draw nourishment from the soil through their roots. *"I am the vine, ye are the branches: He that abideth in me, and I in him, the same bringeth forth much fruit: for without me ye can do nothing"* (John 15:5). Like a branch attached to the vine, we can be **converted** only by staying close to Jesus. Just as He sends sunshine and rain to nurture the tiniest of plants, the Lord of the harvest offers nourishment to each of us, **converting** us into "meet for the master's use" (2 Timothy 2:21).

Accepting Christ as Lord of our lives is just the beginning of our **conversion** and life with Him. We must continue to follow His leadership daily, allowing Him to guide us with our daily problems. This includes recognizing the Holy Spirit's power in us (Acts 1:8); Galatians 5:22), and transforming our lives to the will of the Lord (Romans 12:1, 2).

Conversion has often been likened to the miraculous metamorphosis that takes place as a tadpole changes into a bullfrog, and a caterpillar into a beautiful butterfly.

Conversion in evangelism is just as dynamic as that of the insect and animal world: Christian warriors are out to change the hearts, minds, attitudes, and actions of persons, to a *continuous* turning away from sin. The reason that this turning must be constant is because **conversion** is not a once-for-all experience, rather it is a *process*. We have *all* sinned and come short of the glory of God (Romans 3:23), hence, God's grace and mercy are renewed in us daily (2 Corinthians 4:16).

With childlike faith, we are to believe in, and trust Jesus not only for renewal, but guidance in our daily walk with Him. We must trust God with a child's simplicity and receptivity—always humble and dependent upon Him, and setting our face toward Him in faith. *"Except ye be converted, and become as little children, ye shall not enter into the kingdom of heaven"* (Matthew 18:3).

Besides the **conversion** of individuals, the Church as an institution is certainly a structure that continuously needs to be converted to the lordship of Jesus Christ. Many churches need *reformation* as well as *transformation,* in order to fulfill the Great Commission. They are so driven by the force of activities, programs, and all sorts of other agendas, that they have no appetite for spiritual matters. Members are anorexic and spiritually emaciated. Hell seems to be winning in the Church, so evidently we are not manifesting the power of heaven here on earth.

"According to Jesus' words, the Church is supposed to be the offensive in the world, so hell is not supposed to win. Yet, Satan is steadily winning through lies, intimidation, and countless deceptions. Jesus has also said that He has given us the power to tread upon serpents and scorpions, and over *all* the power of the enemy.[17]

Author Tony Evans, in his book *The Kingdom Agenda*, offers a powerful test for the Church's power on earth: "So the test of our power, both individually and corporately as the body of Christ is whether hell backs up when we show up. If hell is winning, then we are not building Christ's church. Instead, we are building our church using Christ's name."[18] Churches must realize that they are the *only* ones who have been given the keys, the authority, the power, and the access to operate heaven's agenda in a hellish world. *"Upon this rock I will build My church; and the gates of hell shall not prevail against it"* (Matthew 16:18).

Paul spoke to the church at Corinth concerning Kingdom power: *"For the kingdom of God is not in word, but in power"*(1 Corinthians 4:20). What Paul is saying is that the Kingdom of God is to be lived, not just discussed. Do we just talk about Kingdom power, or is there evidence of the power of the Kingdom operating in and through the Church? We can have all the right answers—know all the words to say about Christ and His Kingdom, but still not show that God's power and love are working in us. Our very lives should reflect God's power.

So, in a new definition for evangelism, we can adopt that of Miles: Evangelism is **being**, **doing**, and **telling** the **Gospel** of the **Kingdom of God** in order that, by the power of the **Holy Spirit**, persons and structures may be **converted** to the lordship of Jesus Christ. Miles presents his definition as being three-dimensional.

Evangelism in "3-D"

In regards to the three dimensions of evangelism, Miles explains that what we *are*, along with our *deeds* and our *word*s reveal the three faces of evangelism: **Being** dimension, **Doing** dimension, **Telling** dimension. We evangelize, he claims, through **being** the Good News, **doing** the Good News, **and telling** the Good News, and making disciples is a task which always includes these three aspects of **life, love and lips.**

Being the Good News:

Evangelism is **being** the "salt of the earth," the "light of the world," and the "aroma of Christ." Christians are to be the salt of the earth (Matthew 5:13a), not merely the salt of their church or of their respective community. If we make no effort to affect the world around us, we are of little value to God. Instead of blending in with everyone else, we are to affect them positively, just as salt brings out the best flavor in food. Salt penetrates food, preserves meat, and flavors food; Christians are to penetrate the earth, preserving that which is good, and flavoring every aspect of life. Like salt, Christians are to give taste to the earth, creating a thirst for the Water of life among them.

Jesus tells us that the salt can lose its taste (13b) by lack of use (not used to the glory of God), overuse (burnout), or misuse. Just as the misuse of salt may destroy the health of a human body, the misuse of our "salt" may cause destruction to a part of the of the Body of Christ. Whereas it may be impossible to restore the benefits of the savorless salt used for food, in the Kingdom of God, salt is *recyclable* with the help of the Holy Spirit, our Enabler and Guide.

Jesus told His disciples, *"You are the light of the world"* (v.14), meaning that, if they lived for Him, they would glow like lights, showing others what Christ is like. Likewise, we are the **light of the world**, but only as we reflect the **light of Christ** which shines upon us. *"Let your light so shine before men, that they may see your good works and give glory to your Father who is in heaven"* (v. 16). The Church, also is expected to be a source of light in the world. It can be likened to the moon—which has no light of its own, but reflects the light of the sun. The Church should reflect the light of Christ.

The apostle Paul had seen a light from heaven that was so bright that he was blinded by it (Acts 26:12); when the scales fell from his eyes and they were opened, he was commissioned to open the eyes of those still in darkness: *"To open their eyes, and to turn them from darkness to light, and from the power of Satan unto God, that they may receive forgiveness of sins..."* (v. 18). So is the mission of the new people of God, the Church, *"to declare the wonderful deeds of him who called you out of darkness into his marvelous light"* (1 Peter 2:9b).

In evangelism, Christians are to be the **light of the world** spiritually, geographically, and vocationally. W. Randall Lolley, president of Southeastern Baptist Theological Seminary, expressed his conversion in terms of lamp lighting: "It was as if the Lord turned on the light in my young life. What had been dark and scary now became bright and peaceful. I was aglow on the inside of my life—saved, forgiven, redeemed, died for!"[19]

In my personal testimony to being taken from darkness to light, I recall seeing things that were apparently always "there," but had been "blinded" to. The greatest illumination for me was being able to "see" God's character, love, and wisdom throughout His Word—with a greater interest and understanding. Prior to becoming saved, I would attempt to read the Bible, but I could never go beyond Noah and the flood without becoming intimidated and frustrated, trying to connect or relate one book to another. Once I dedicated my life to the Lord, I began reading His Word with a passion unending. Much of the new "light" guiding my walk came from the "fire" that began to burn within me, and now, I cannot withhold it—I must "run and tell it!" The prophet, Jeremiah described his experience as *"a burning fire shut up in my bones"* (Jeremiah 20:9).

Besides being the salt of the earth and the light of the world, believers are to be a like a sweet perfume (savor) whose fragrance others cannot help but notice. To some, it is good news; but to others, it is repulsive: *"Now thanks be to God, which always causeth us to triumph in Christ, and maketh manifest the savour of his knowledge by us in every place. For we are unto God a sweet savour of Christ, in them that are saved, and in them that perish"* (2 Corinthians 2:15).

To some who were at first dead (unsaved) in their trespasses, the Gospel becomes a sweet, life-giving aroma of life (Christ) unto life (eternal life), as it quickens them, making them more lively and joyous. Unto others (who reject the Gospel), it is a smell of death (spiritual) unto death (eternal). As Christians, we cannot control a person's opinion or reaction to our Gospel message, no more than we can control their opinion about a perfume's fragrance. However, if we remain true to Christ—reflecting His character in every aspect of our lifestyle, His Spirit working in us will attract others, just as a pleasant fragrance does.

"Next time you think of evangelism, bring to your mind the sweetest most pleasant smell you can recall. That wonderful fragrance is evangelism. You and I and the rest of Christ's disciples are the perfume which makes the world smell good. Any stinking odor which we give off, any stench which we may have, belongs to the old nature and is not a part of the new creation."[20] In short, we must bear the fragrance of the knowledge of God—being the aroma of Christ *everywhere*. We are to not only live differently, act differently, speak differently, and think differently, but also "smell" differently.

Doing the Good News:

Doing the Good News involves fishing for persons, **bearing fruit** that remains, and engaging in the ministry of reconciliation). As Jesus was walking by the Sea of Galilee, He spotted two brothers, Simon and Andrew, casting a net into the sea. He said to them, *"Follow me and I will make you become fishers of men"* (Matthew 4:19). William F. Arndt and F. Wilbur Gingrich, two Greek Scholars say that Jesus was perhaps "allegorically connecting their present and future vocations."[21] In other words, Jesus was telling them that "from now on, you'll be catching men instead of catching fish."

Jesus was both calling Simon and Andrew to discipleship, and to follow Him, allowing Him to make them "fishers of men." Jesus was calling these men away from their productive trade (fishing) to be productive spiritually—to fish for souls. His call motivated them to get up and leave their jobs immediately. Unlike the response of some, neither man made an excuse as to why it wasn't a good time to go. That's the total dedication Jesus wants from us, not half-hearted commitment.

On the way to Jerusalem, Jesus explained the cost of **doing** the Good News to three different men. One man said unto Jesus: "Lord, I will follow thee whithersoever thou goest" (Luke 9:57). Jesus' response to him was, *"Foxes have holes, and birds of the air have nests; but the Son of man hath not where to lay his head"* (v. 58). As Jesus said to another, *"Follow me"* (v. 59), this man's excuse was that he needed to bury his father. Jesus told him, *"Let the dead bury their dead: but go thou and preach the kingdom of God"* (v. 60).

The dialogue between Jesus and a third man reinforces the fact that workers in the Kingdom cannot pick and choose among Jesus' work and follow Him selectively. When the man said to Jesus, *"Lord, I will follow thee; but let me first go bid them farewell, which are at home at my house"* (v. 61). Jesus said to him, NO MAN, HAVING PUT HIS HAND TO THE PLOUGH, AND LOOKING BACK, IS FIT FOR THE KINGDOM OF GOD" (v. 62).

In following Jesus, we have to accept the *cross* along with the *crown*; no cross, no crown! Paul's comfort, as he went through suffering and faced death, was: *"For if we be dead with him, we shall also live with him: if we suffer, we shall also reign with him: if we deny him, he also will deny us"* (2 Timothy 2:11-12). God promises us a wonderful future with Him, a life eternal, if we share in the suffering of Kingdom building, always striving to be fruitful branches in His vineyard.

Doing the Good News includes **bearing fruit,** as we are the branches of the true Vine. Jesus Christ is the True Vine, believers are the branches of this Vine, and God the Father is the Husbandman of the vineyard (John 15:1, 5). In the Old Testament, grapes were symbolic of Israel's fruitfulness in doing God's work on earth (Psalm 80:8; Isaiah 51:1-7; Ezekiel 19:10-14). At the Passover meal, the fruit of the vine symbolized God's goodness to His people.

The fruitful branches (true believers) in God's vineyard (the Church) live in union with Christ, and produce much fruit; but those who turn back from following Christ will be separated from the Vine. They are as good as dead, and will be cut off and cast aside. Thus, anyone who tries to block the efforts of God's followers will also be cut off from the Vine. *"Every branch in me beareth not fruit he taketh away: and every branch that beareth fruit, he purgeth it, that it may bring forth more fruit"* (v. 2).

From a grapevine, we look for grapes, and from Christians, we look for Christianity; the fruit of Christianity is none other than Christian temper and disposition, a Christian lifestyle and conversation. We also **bear fruit** by honoring God and by doing good. One law of nature is that everything produces after its kind. Apple trees bear apples. Peach trees bear peaches. Horses bear horses. So it stands to reason that Christians should bear Christians; hence, if we do not grow and produce after our kind, it is questionable whether we are really Christians.

Christians are told to **bear fruit** that will forever remain: *"Ye have not chosen me, but I have chosen you, and ordained you, that ye shall go and bring forth fruit, and that your fruit should remain"* (v. 16). Whereas fruit that we store up here on earth will perish, any fruit which we bear in doing the will of God will forever remain, because we are abiding in Christ.

The ministry of reconciliation, which God has entrusted to us, is also a part of **doing** the Good News in evangelism. God was in Christ reconciling the world to Himself, and has made us ambassadors for Christ.

Telling the Good News:

The **telling** dimension of evangelism is: the proclamation of the Gospel; bearing witness to Jesus Christ; and advertising the wonderful deeds of God in Christ.

Proclamation of the Gospel - In His own hometown, and before His own people, Jesus Christ proclaimed His own Gospel—the Good News, that forgiveness of sins and eternal life are available to all people, because of His own life, death, burial, and resurrection.

Proclaiming Himself to be the One who would bring this to pass, and as all eyes were on Him, Jesus boldly states, "The Spirit of the Lord is upon me, because he hath anointed me to preach the gospel to the poor; he hath sent me to heal the brokenhearted, to preach deliverance to the captives, and recovering of sight to the blind; to set at liberty them that are bruised, to preach the acceptable year of the Lord" (Luke 4:18-19). Jesus let the crowd know that He was fitted (anointed) for the undertaking, and had been called (sent) to do it: "This day is this Scripture fulfilled in your ears" (v.21).

Christians have been commissioned to proclaim the exact same message (the Gospel) to the exact same people (the poor of the world). The "poor" are those poor in spirit, the meek, the humble, and to those who are truly sorrowful for sin, and the Gospel is to be preached not only to their ears, but to their hearts as well.

CHAPTER 5

"THESE TWELVE JESUS SENT FORTH"

God can and does use anyone to serve Him in a special way, no matter how significant he or she appears. He uses ordinary people to do His extraordinary work. It has been said that when God chooses to do an "impossible" thing, he takes an ordinary man and crushes him. Jesus, the Son of God ministered to thousands, but He poured His life into twelve men, giving them intense training, and ordaining them to preach His Kingdom.

The twelve disciples represented a wide range of backgrounds and life experiences, and many had no more leadership ability than those not chosen.

Jesus based His selections not on the men's talents and abilities, but on their willingness to obey Him, and follow Him with a willing heart. He called people from all walks of life: fishermen (Peter, James, John, Andrew, Philip) a tax collector (Matthew), a fierce patriot (Simon the Zealot), etc. There were common men as well as leaders, rich men as well as poor, educated and uneducated. Jesus "called" these men, he didn't "draft" them or force them—or even ask for volunteers. They had to be willing to say and do what seemed strange to the world, to give when others were "taking," and to love when others chose to hate.

Despite their confusion, faltering faith, and misunderstandings during Jesus' lifetime, the disciples became powerful witnesses to His resurrection, leaving all believers the perfect blueprint for yielding to the Holy Spirit for power, strength, courage and insight, in order to witness for Christ throughout the entire world. The story of these powerful men does not end with the Gospels, but continues in the book of Acts and many of the epistles.

SIMON PETER

<u>Background and Profile</u>: a bi-lingual Jew was also named Cephas and Peter, both names meaning "Rock." In partnership with his brother, Andrew, in the fishing business on the Sea of Galilee. Had some providential preparation for later missionary preaching: promptly left his boat and net to follow Jesus (Matthew 4:18). Always named first in lists of disciples of Jesus.

<u>His Strengths</u>: Became the recognized leader among Jesus' disciples; one of the "inner group" of the three. The first great voice of the Gospel both during and after Pentecost. Wrote 1 and 2 Peter. Bold, daring—definitely a man of action!

<u>His Weaknesses</u>: Brash and impulsive, often speaking without thinking. Denied three times that he even knew Jesus. Found it hard to treat Gentile Christians as equals.

<u>Gospel Performance</u>: Peter's first contact with Jesus was in Judea, near the place where John the Baptist was carrying on his ministry. He had come to hear John, and became his disciple. Peter was quick to take the initiative; he volunteered to go to Jesus on the water (Matthew 14:28), but his faith wavered when he took his eyes off Jesus. Very often Peter acted or spoke for the entire group of disciples; at

Caesarea Philippi, Peter was the spokesman in affirming Jesus as the Messiah: *"And Simon Peter answered and said, Thou art the Christ, the Son of the living God"* (Matthew 16:16).

When Jesus announced His impending suffering and death, Peter rebuked Him. He also spoke for the other disciples concerning future rewards, reminding Jesus of their (the disciples) sacrifice in following Jesus; he thus asked Jesus what their reward would be. Jesus reminded Peter of what they all would gain—both in the present life as well as eternally (Luke 18:28). We, too, learn from this discussion that we can never out give God; what we gain in following Christ is worth far more than we could ever "sacrifice."

The Kingdom of God must always be our focus: *"But seek ye first the kingdom of God and His righteousness, and all these things shall be added unto you"* (Matthew 6:33).

Though Peter often stumbled, i.e., speaking out of turn, finding it difficult at first to treat Gentile Christians as equal. Though he thrice denied knowing Jesus, he never failed to follow Him, and was the first great voice of the Gospel to be heard at Pentecost *"But Peter, standing up with the eleven, lifted up his voice, and said unto them...this is that which is spoken by the prophet Joel...it shall come to pass...I will pour out my Spirit upon all flesh...I will show wonders of heaven...signs in the earth...that whosoever shall call upon the name of the Lord shall be saved"* (Acts 2:14-21).

When much of the crowd was in doubt, and thinking that the disciples were drunk, Peter preached the Good News about Jesus Christ; and three thousand souls were saved! (v. 41). Peter wrote two epistles (1 Peter and 2 Peter), the first addressing the Christians' behavior under the pressures of suffering; the second offering encouragement to the suffering Christians and to challenge them to continue living holy lives.

Peter is a perfect example of how a warm-hearted,

gifted, impulsive and imperfect person can be won by love, molded through discipline, training, and even hardships—to be used by God to do great things for Him. Jesus' first words to Peter were, *"Come ye after me"* (Mark 1:17), and His last words to him were, *"Follow thou me"* (John 21:22); and follow Him Peter did.

Lessons from Peter's Life: God's faithfulness can compensate for man's greatest unfaithfulness. It is better to be a follower of Jesus who fails than one who fails to follow Him. Enthusiasm must be backed up by faith and understanding; otherwise, it fails.

JAMES, SON OF ZEBEDEE

Background and Profile: Elder brother of John, the apostle; one of the Lord's earliest disciples; a fisherman in partnership with his brother John, Peter, and Andrew. Along with the latter three, James became a special confidant of Jesus.

His Strengths: Deeply committed to Jesus; ambitious; one of an inner circle of 3.

His Weaknesses: Selfish, judgmental, and short-tempered (known for two outbursts–Luke 9:54).

Gospel Prominence: James witnessed the raising of Jairus' daughter (Mark 5:37). He was at the transfiguration (Matthew 17:1-8) and at the agony in the Garden of Gethsemane (Matthew 26:36-46). Along with his brother, John, James received the surname Boanerges, or "Sons of Thunder." An example of their "thunder" was when they asked for Jesus' approval to call down fire from heaven to consume the inhabitants of the Samaritan village that had refused to allow Jesus and His apostles to pass through on their way to Jerusalem (Mark 3:17).

There were times when the eagerness and self-seeking nature of James and John angered the other apostles, such as when they wanted the highest positions in Jesus' Kingdom. Jesus reminded them that true greatness comes in serving others, not in personal glory (Mark 10:41). On Tuesday of Passion Week, James was one of the four who asked Jesus the question concerning last things, i.e., when the Temple would be destroyed. Jesus gave them a prophetic picture of *that* as well as other future events connected with His return to earth (Mark 13:3-4). James was present when the risen Lord appeared at the Sea of Tiberius (John 21:1-14). He was the first martyr among the apostles, being put to death by King Herod Agrippa I, in about A.D. 44, shortly after Herod's own death (Acts 12:2).

Lesson from James' Life: The loss of one's life is not too great a price for following Jesus.

JOHN, SON OF ZEBEDEE

Background and Profile: A fisherman on the Sea of Galilee; first a disciple of John the Baptist, then of Jesus; called himself, "the disciple whom Jesus loved."

His Strengths: Ambitious; grew to be very loving. Third disciple in the core group; closest to Jesus.

His Weaknesses: Judgmental; tendency (like his brother, James) to outbursts of selfishness and anger. Asked for a special position in Jesus' Kingdom.

Gospel Prominence: John had heeded the call to repentance and baptism, in preparation of the coming Messiah (John 1:35-39). Jesus appeared by the Sea of Galilee, and called Peter, Andrew, James, and John from their fishing to be with Him constantly—to be trained to become fishers of men (Mark 4:18-22). Like his brother, James, John had a tendency to outbursts of selfishness and anger, but Jesus knew him well, and loved him fully. John 13:23; 21:20).

John was one of the three most prominent of the apostles closest to Jesus. He observed Jesus' first miracle, at the wedding in Cana (John 2:1-9), the cleansing of the Temple (2:15), Jesus' dialogue with Nicodemus (3:1-21), and the raising of Jairus' daughter (Mark 5:37). John was present at the Transfiguration (Matthew 17:1), and was sent, with Peter, by Jesus to make ready the Passover (Luke 22:8). At the Passover, John asked Jesus (leaning on His breast) who His betrayer would be (John 13:25).

Although John fled (as did the other apostles) when Jesus was captured (Matthew 26:56), he got up the courage to be present at the trial of Jesus. He also stood near the Cross on which Jesus was nailed. Jesus commissioned John to look after his mother (John 19:6). John also went with Peter to see, for themselves the empty grave of Jesus (20: 2-3). John was the first to recognize Jesus in the appearance of the risen Lord (21:1-7), and after the Ascension, remained in Jerusalem with the other apostles, praying and waiting for the coming of the Comforter, the Holy Spirit (Acts 1:12-13).

Lesson from John's Life: When God changes one's life, He does not take away personality traits—He channels them into more effective service for Him. John wrote five New Testament books: the *Gospel of John; 1 John, 2 John, 3 John and Revelation.*

John wrote his Gospel to prove conclusively that Jesus *is* the Son of God, and that all who believe in Him will have eternal life. In John's Gospel, eight specific signs or miracles that show: the nature of Jesus' power and love; His power over everything created; and His love of *all* people.

ANDREW

Background and Profile: Brother of Simon Peter, and a fisherman. John the Baptist directed Andrew to Jesus as the Lamb of God. When Andrew accepted John the Baptist's testimony about Jesus, he went immediately to tell his brother, Simon, thus bringing *him*, also, to Jesus. Eager to bring others to Christ.

Gospel Prominence: Andrew was appointed by Jesus to be an apostle (Matthew 10:2), and his name is always next to Philip's when listing the apostles. Andrew was with

Philip when he expressed doubt that the multitude could be fed with the five loaves of bread and two fishes (John 6:6-11). Andrew was one of the four who asked Jesus about the destruction of the Temple, and also the *time* of the Second Advent (Mark 13:3) After the book of Acts, Andrew is never mentioned again, but he is remembered as one who was eager to bring others to Jesus. It is believed that Andrew preached at Scythia, and suffered martyrdom in Achaia, being crucified on an X shaped cross, which is now called a St. Andrew" cross.[22]

PHILIP

Background and Profile: a disciple to John the Baptist; often referred to as the Apostle Philip—to distinguish between him and Philip the Evangelist and Philip the Deacon; close friend of Andrew and Peter; timid, retiring; questioning attitude.

Gospel Prominence: The dialogue between Philip and Jesus (John 14:8) shows Philip's reluctance to believe whole-heartedly in the Kingdom. At times he appeared to have difficulty in grasping its meaning, a factor in Jesus' asking of him, *"How are we to buy bread so that this people can eat"* (6:5-6). It is possible that Jesus was testing Philip's faith and growth. Philip was from Bethsaida (1:44), a town only nine miles away; if anyone knew where to get food, it was he. To strengthen Philip's faith, Jesus was asking for a human solution (knowing that there was none) to prelude the miracle that he was about to perform.

Though Philip was a Jew, he had a Greek name, and thus served as a contact person for the Greeks; he was successful in bringing Gentiles to Jesus (12:20-23). In fact, Philip brought Nathaniel to Jesus: *"Can there any good thing come out of Nazareth? Philip said to him, Come and see......Nathaniel answered and saith, Rabbi, thou art the Son of God; thou art the King of Israel"* (1:46-49P).

NATHANIEL (BARTHOLOMEW)

Nathaniel is mentioned in all the synoptic Gospels as Bartholomew, but in the Gospel of John, as Nathaniel (Matthew 10:3; Mark 3:18; Luke 6:14; John 1:45). Some scholars believe that Bartholomew is the surname of Nathaniel.

If Nathaniel had based his actions on his prejudices, he would have *missed* the opportunity to know and be of service to the Messiah. Like the Jews, Nathaniel despised anyone coming out of Nazareth. But he was honest and straightforward; when Philip told him to "come see," Nathaniel acknowledged Jesus as the Son of God and King of Israel (see profile on Philip, above).

MATTHEW

Background and Profile: A tax collector; hence, a despised outcast of the Jews, because of his dishonest character. Also called Levi (Luke 5:27); the son of Alphaeus Mark 2:14).

His Strengths: Responded immediately to Jesus' call, abandoning his corrupt (but financially profitable) way of life to follow Jesus. Invited Jesus to a party with his notorious friends. Wrote the Gospel of Matthew.

His Weaknesses: Like many of the other tax collectors, had a reputation for cheating, overcharging, and support of Rome.

Gospel Prominence: While in his career as a tax collector, Matthew had no clue that the very skills that made him such an astute record keeper in his secular profession, would one day enable him to record: the greatest Life ever lived; the most highly valued and widely read account of the four Gospels in the early church; and the most quoted Gospel in Christian literature before A.D. 180. Matthew's readiness to follow Jesus makes some scholars think that perhaps he had come into contact with Jesus before, and had already decided to dedicate his life to *His* cause.

Whereas some of the other disciples had their fishing careers to return to, Matthew knew that he would face unemployment, and there was no turning back, once he decided to follow Jesus. Matthew's concern for his former colleagues—whom he invited to dinner at his home (Luke 5:29-32), leaves one to believe that he was a man of deep spiritual conviction, for his intent seemed to have been to win the men to Christ.

To prove that Jesus is the Messiah, Matthew connects the Old Testament with the New Testament, with emphasis on the fulfillment of prophecy: from the birth and preparation of Jesus the *King* (Matthew 4:12-25), to the death, burial, and resurrection of Jesus the *King* (26:1-28:29). The final chapters of Matthew focus on Jesus' final days on earth: the Last Supper (265:20); His prayer in Gethsemane (vv. 36-44); the betrayal of Judas (vv47-49); the flight of the disciples (v. 56); Peter's denial of Christ (vv. 69-75); the trials before Caiaphas and Pilate (27:11-26); His final words on the Cross (45-50); and His burial in a borrowed tomb (27:57).

Lesson from Matthew's Life: God has no less meaningful purpose for one of His children than the other, and consistently accepts people from *every* level of society. From the beginning, each of is one of God's works in progress, as He trusts us with skills and abilities ahead of schedule.

THOMAS

Background and Profile: Also called Didymus, his surname (John 1:16).

His Strengths: Courageous; just as intense in his belief as his doubts. Loyal and honest.

His Weaknesses: Along with the others, abandoned Jesus at His arrest; refused to believe the others' claims to have seen Christ, and demanded proof. Struggled with a pessimistic outlook.

Gospel Prominence: The disciples knew the danger of going to Bethany with Jesus so they tried to talk Jesus out of going—all but Thomas. In his bravery, Thomas expressed what all of them felt: *"Let us also go, that we may die with him"* (John 11:8, 16). Thomas did not hesitate to follow Jesus! Thomas is often remembered as "Doubting Thomas," but he deserves to be respected for his faith. Thomas' doubts had purpose to them—he only wanted the truth, hence, doubting was merely his way of responding, not his way of life. Despite what he felt, Thomas struggled to be faithful to his Lord, and loyal to the believers.

Because Thomas was not with the other disciples when Jesus presented Himself on the evening of the Resurrection, he refused to believe that He had risen. Eight days later, Thomas was with the group when Jesus came again. Not even his ten colleagues could change Thomas' mind about their witness to the resurrection of Jesus until he saw for himself. Knowing Thomas' faith, and understanding his skepticism, Jesus invited Thomas to personally witness all proof of His resurrection: *"Reach hither thy finger, and behold my hands; and reach hither thy hand, and thrust it into my side: and be not faithless, but believing. And Thomas answered and said unto him, My Lord and my God"* (20:27).

In John 21:1-8, Thomas is with six other apostles at the Sea of Galilee when Jesus showed Himself for the third time. He is also in the Upper Room at Jerusalem after the Ascension (Acts 1:13). Tradition has it that Thomas carried on Christ's work in Parthia, Persia, and India. A place near Madras is called St. Thomas' Mount.

Lessons from Thomas' Life: It is better to doubt "out loud" than to disbelieve in silence; Thomas didn't stay with his doubt, but allowed Jesus to bring him to belief. Doubt can encourage rethinking, when used more to sharpen one's mind, rather than to change it.

Thomas *wanted* to believe that Jesus was risen—but he searched for more evidence, which brought him to the truth.

James

Background and Profile: A child of Joseph and Mary; the Lord's half-brother, and not a believer during the Lord's lifetime; did not accept Jesus as the Messiah.

Gospel Prominence: A witness to Christ's resurrection (1 Corinthians 15:7), which seemed to transform him into a believer and a disciple. James was in the Upper Room (Acts 1:14), and became a pillar of the Church at Jerusalem (Acts 12:17; 15:4-34; 21:18; Galatians 2:1-10). He earned the name "James the Just" for his piety, and the name "The Man with Camel's Knees because of his belief in the power of prayer (also evidenced in his epistle bearing his name). James was cruelly martyred by the Scribes and Pharisees, who cast him from the pinnacle of the Temple. When the fall did not kill him, they finally stoned him to death. There is a sepulcher called "The Tomb of St. James" located across the Valley of Jehoshaphat.

Thaddaeus

Thaddaeus is also called Labbeus or Lebbeus, and sometimes identified as Jude, who wrote the epistle bearing his name. Some hold that he is the son of or possibly the brother of James the Just. Thaddaeus is only mentioned in two of the four lists of apostles, Matthew 10:3, and Mark 3:18.

SIMON, THE ZEALOT

A fierce patriot, Simon the Zealot was a member of a radical political party, working for the violent overthrow of Roman rule in Israel. Luke refers to him as Simon Zelotes (Luke 6:15; Acts 1:13). Simon had to give up his aggressive, revolutionary plans, when he decided to follow Jesus and become one of His disciples.

JUDAS ISCARIOT

<u>Background and Profile</u>: Only non-Galilean. Treacherous and greedy. A Thief (John 12:6). *Pretended* to be concerned for the poor, when it was really covetousness. Kept the money bag for the expense of the group. Was able to recognize the evil in his betrayal of Jesus. He was the only disciple who never called Jesus "Lord," he called Him "Master."

<u>Weaknesses and Mistakes</u>: With the other disciples, shared a persistent misunderstanding of Jesus' mission. Betrayed Jesus. Committed suicide instead of seeking forgiveness.

<u>Gospel Prominence</u>: When Jesus kept talking about dying, all of His disciples had varying degrees of fear, anger, and disappointment. None understood why they had been chosen—if Jesus' mission was "doomed to fail." They all expected Jesus to start a political rebellion and overthrow Rome. As treasurer, Judas assumed that he would have a similar high position in the new Kingdom. Judas' anxieties catapulted him to a new but devastating height—placing him in a position where Satan could manipulate him. He became very indignant when Mary of Bethany anointed Jesus with her very expensive perfume. Judas considered it waste (Mark 14:4-5).

Jesus' praise of Mary's sacrifice on His behalf was more than Judas' could take, so he immediately went to the chief of priests to prepare for the betrayal—to hand Jesus over to them. Judas sold Christ for thirty pieces of silver (Matthew 26:14-16), but when he realized that Jesus was condemned to death, repented himself, saying, *"I have betrayed the innocent blood"* (27:4). Judas tried to give the money back, but his deed was irreversible. Judas *chose* to hang himself, rather than truly repent and ask forgiveness.

<u>Lesson from Judas' Life</u>: The consequences of evil are devastating; evil motives leave us open to being used by Satan for even greater evil. [Although Judas' betrayal was a

part of God's sovereign plan (Psalm 41:9; Zechariah 11:12-13; Matthew 20:18; Acts 1:16), we cannot call him a "puppet" of God's will. Judas made the *choice*. God knew what that choice would be and confirmed it.]

SUMMARY

One does not need fame or fortune to love, serve, and sit with God, for He alone chooses workers and leaders by His standards, not ours. A person's background does not prevent God from working powerfully in his or her life. God uses us in spite of what we see as our limitations and failures. Jesus, God's Son, called each of the disciples to follow Him; He didn't ask them to volunteer, nor did He draft them or force them—He *called* them, and they immediately obeyed. They didn't make excuses as to why it wasn't a "good time" for them to go. When we are asked to serve the Lord, we, too must do it at once. God is faithful to those who obey Him—and *His* timing is *perfect*.

CHAPTER 6

"THE SAME COMMIT THOU TO FAITHFUL MEN"

If the Church consistently followed the advice which Paul gave to Timothy in his "last will and testament," regarding the foundations of a Christian, two things might happen: 1) geometrical expansion; 2) there would be more spiritually qualified workers for Christ. *"And the things thou has heard of me among many witnesses, the same commit thou to faithful men, who shall be able to teach others also"* (2 Timothy 2:2). . Well taught believers can teach others, hence, disciples need to be *equipped* in order to *pass on* their faith. Until new believers are telling others the Good News that they have learned, the Church's work is incomplete.

Paul saw potential in his "son of faith," Timothy, and decided to invest his own life in training him properly for evangelism. Three words or phrases in Paul's instructions to Timothy reveal much for us to draw upon: *commit, faithful men,* and *teach others also.*

Commit: We become like the people we associate. Paul had transmitted not only what he knew, but also what he *was* as a person to Timothy. Now he's more or less saying to him, "whatever I have invested in you, now you must transmit this, as a disciple-maker to *faithful men*, thereby making new disciples."

Faithful men: God still seeks out faithful men and women whose hearts are perfect toward Him: *"For the eyes of the Lord run to and fro throughout the whole earth, to shew himself strong in the behalf of them whose heart is perfect toward him"* The person that is *faithful* has: adopted as his or her objective in life the same objective which God sets forth in His Word: *"But seek ye first the kingdom of God, and His righteousness; and all these things shall be added unto you"* (Matthew 6:33). This means placing the Kingdom over you family, your possessions, health, dreams, goals, your vocation—everything!

The *faithful* person is willing to pay *any* price to have the will of God fulfilled in his or her life: *"thou therefore endure hardness, as a good soldier of Jesus Christ...that he may please Him who hath chosen him..."* (2 Timothy 2:3-4). In other words, the faithful steadfastly resist becoming ensnared in the world's glittering enticements. All that makes up you must belong to Christ, who must be free to do with you and take from you what He wills. God owns everything anyway: *"For every beast of the forest is mine, and the cattle on a thousand hills...for the world is mine, and the fulness thereof"* (Psalm 50:10, 12).

The *faithful* person has a love for the Word of God. The prophet, Jeremiah said that he found the words of the Lord and that they were such a joy to him that he "ate" them (Jeremiah 15:16). Job said that the Word of God was more important to him than his necessary food: *"I have esteemed the words of His mouth more than my necessary food"* (Job 23:12). By His grace, I now have an insatiable appetite for the Word of God, and am trying daily, moment by moment, to be in submission to its authority.

A servant heart is what the *faithful* person has—one that

is not above doing any job listed in Kingdom building. As workers for the Kingdom, we cannot afford to allow our positions or titles in the church prevent us from working in unity with others. In teaching His disciples, Jesus spoke against those who enjoy being served and exercising authority over others: *"But it shall not be so among you: but whosoever will be great among you, let him be your minister, and whosoever will be chief among you, let him be your servant: even as the Son of man came not to be ministered to, but to minister, and to give his life a ransom for many"* (Matthew 20:26-28).

Some leaders find it hard to serve those "under" them. Jesus put action to His own words when He washed His disciples' feet. (John 13). When the disciples, especially Peter, had a problem with their Lord acting as a "servant boy," Jesus said to them, *" If I then, your Lord and Master, have washed your feet, ye also ought to wash one another's feet. For I have given you an example, that ye should do as I have done to you...the servant is not greater than his lord;* neither *he that is sent greater than he that sent him"* (14-16).

To be *faithful*, one must love people as God loves them: *"Beloved, let us love one another; for love is of God....Herein is love...that he sent his Son to be a propitiation for our sins"* (1 John 4:10). The *faithful* person has a love for people, and will therefore get involved in their lives. Granted, everyone is not a "people" person; but John isn't telling us how *many* people we must love, rather how *much* to love the people God has and will give us to love. When He sees that we are ready to faithfully love people, not only will He bring them to us, but will also strengthen us to do what He asks.

Finally, the *faithful* person has learned to *discipline* his own life; after all, the word disciple comes from the root word, discipline. In Paul's letter to the church at Corinth, he likened the Christian journey to that of running a race— that it takes hard work, grueling preparation and self-denial:

"Know ye not that they which run in a race run all, but one receiveth the prize? So run, that ye may obtain. And every man that striveth for the mastery is temperate in all things. Now they do it to obtain a corruptible crown; but we an incorruptible. I therefore so run, not as uncertainly; so fight I, not as one that beteath the air: but I keep under my body, and bring it into subjection: lest that by any means, when I have preached to others, I myself should be a castaway" (1 Corinthians 9:24-27).

Paul's entire message here is about purpose and discipline. As believers, we are running toward our heavenly reward, and there are essential disciplines that help us to run our race with vigor and stamina: Bible study, prayer, and worship.

To remain *faithful*, we must also have no confidence in the flesh (2 Corinthians 1:9; Romans 7:18). Having confidence in the flesh borders on embracing the characteristics of worldliness (living as though you have no need for God). A good way to test how much confidence we have in the flesh is to take an inventory of how much we use the words "me," "my," and "I" in our own conversations. If we want to be God's instruments to communicate and work with other people, we must be willing to subjugate our own ideas for the sake of the whole team.

Teach others also: "Teaching others also" falls under the heading, *multiplicative process*, which is the only way that Christ's Commission can ever be ultimately fulfilled.

Teaching others to disciple entails the imparting of a life (Paul to Timothy), and cannot be done solely within the confines of a classroom. The principles of the multiplicative process, and how it works will be discussed in chapter eight.

As Paul continues to teach Timothy on discipleship, he was straightforward about hardships and suffering that he would face, but could expect to endure: *"Thou therefore endure hardness, as a good soldier of Jesus Christ...and if a* man strive for masteries, yet he is not crowned, except he strive lawfully. The husbandman that laboureth must be first partaker of the fruits...and the Lord give thee understanding in all things" (2 Timothy 2:3-7).

Paul's point is this: Good soldiers, good athletes, and good farmers keep going despite suffering, because of the thought of *victory*! Like soldiers, Christians have to give up worldly security and endure rigorous discipline; like athletes, Christians must train hard and follow the rules; like farmers, Christians must work extremely hard, hoping for a good harvest. The bottom line is to keep our eyes on the *prize*—glorifying God, winning others to Christ, and one day living eternally with our Creator and Sustainer.

As our Lord Jesus advanced His disciples to the degree and dignity of apostles, His *ordination* sermon looked further than to their initial mission: the services they were to do, methods they would employ, the miracles they would work, and how they were to conduct themselves; it also prepared them for the *rejection* many of them would experience by being Christians. Jesus thoroughly forewarned them of the troubles they should meet with, when, after His resurrection, their commission would be greatly enlarged. Jesus told the apostles not only *what* they should suffer, and *from whom*, but He also counseled them as to what course to take when *persecution* came.

Jesus tells His disciples what they should suffer, and from whom: *"Behold, I send you forth as sheep in the midst of wolves: be ye therefore wise as serpents, and harmless as doves. But beware of men: for they will deliver you up to the councils....scourge you in their synagogues....brought before governors and kings for my sake, for a testimony against the Gentiles. But when they deliver you up take no thought how or what ye shall speak: for it shall be given you in theat same hour what ye shall speak. For it is not ye that speak, but the Spirit of your Father which speaketh in you"*

(Matthew 10:16-19).

The things that the disciples were to avoid were clear and precise: anything that gave advantage to their enemies; meddling with worldly or political concerns: appearances of evil, selfishness, or underhand measures. As with the disciples, Christ has dealt fairly and faithfully with us, not wanting anything to come as a surprise to us, yet assuring us of victory in Him: *"These things I have spoken unto you, that in me ye might have peace. In the world ye shall have tribulation: but be of good cheer; I have overcome the world"* (John 16:33). We must always remember that Jesus does not abandon us to our struggles, and nothing happens to us that he has not already faced and conquered.

In spite of the inevitable struggles we face in this life, we are not alone. The ultimate victory has already been won at Calvary (Matthew 27:50), thus, we can claim the peace of Christ in the most troublesome times. It behooves us to remember the words in Isaiah 54:17: *"No weapon that is formed against you shall prosper, and every tongue that accuses you in judgment you will condemn. This is the heritage of the servants of the Lord, and their vindication is from Me, declares the Lord."*

Knowing these truths will keep men and women from entering discipleship training with their heads in the clouds. The minute we each said "yes" to Jesus, we became bloodstained targets for the Enemy. The Christian walk is not easy, for there will always be obstacles to overcome. In the middle of Paul's conversion experience, Jesus gave Paul (through Ananias), a glimpse of what would be waiting for him down th road: *"Go thy way: for he is a chosen vessel unto to me to bear my name before the Gentiles, and kings, and the children of Israel; for I will show him how great things he must suffer for my name's sake"* (Acts 9:15-16).

There is a tremendous cost in following Christ, specifically in the categories of family, government, and even religion, as people's values, morals, goals, and purposes will differ. Christian commitment often separates friends and loved ones, but regardless, Jesus commands wholehearted devotion and commitment from us. *"And a man's foes should be they of his own household. He that loveth his father and mother more than me is not worthy of me: and he that loveth son or daughter more than me is not worthy of me. And he that taketh not his cross, and followeth after me, is not worthy of me. He that findeth his life shall lose it: and he that loseth his life for my sake shall find it"* (Matthew 10:36-39).

In this passage, Jesus is not telling us to hate anyone, rather, we must not hold anyone above Him. Our first love and commitment is His—He earned it with His precious blood. Any loved one that we have are "on loan" to us, and we are mere vessels through which God will love them. Our love for family cannot be self-serving, or used as an excuse to not serve God or do His work. The more we love and cling to this life's treasures (money, power, popularity), the more we stand to forfeit our eternal rewards.

A certain man, who *thought* that he was ready to follow Jesus, said that he would follow Jesus wherever He would go. Jesus clearly let this man know that he didn't have a clue as to the hardships of following Him: *"Foxes have holes, and birds of the air have nests, but the Son of man hath not where to lay his head"* (Luke 9:58). Another man of whom Jesus *asked* to "follow Him," said that he must first bury his father. Jesus told him to *"Let the dead bury their dead: but go thou and preach the kingdom of God"* (v. 60).

The first word "dead" in Jesus' statement refers to the *spiritually dead.* Jesus' reply to a third man, who volunteers to follow Him—but first must "bid farewell to guests at his home, is one that specifically applies to those who are already working in the vineyard: *"No man, having put his hand to the plough, and looking back, is fit for the kingdom of God"* (v. 62). When working in God's Kingdom, it sometimes becomes difficult, dealing with the various personalities, backgrounds, and "hidden" agendas of people. Frequently we may be tempted to "pull out," or stagger in our own commitment. But we must stay focused on our overall purpose—the edification of the Body of Christ.

As Christians, we must each ask ourselves several questions: "Who am I really working for?" "Who deserves the glory here, me or the Lord?" "Is there anything between me and God?; Are there any sins that I have been unwilling to confess and forsake?; Are there any areas of my life that I have not placed under God's control?; Do my financial assets belong to Him? How about my "things" (possessions)? Scripture tells us that people who mind earthly things are enemies of the Cross of Christ: *"For many walk, of whom I have told you often, and now tell you even weeping, that they are the enemies of the cross of Christ: whose end is destruction, whose God is their belly, and whose glory is in their shame, who mind earthly things"* (Philippians 3:18-19).

A *rich* young man, once, came running and kneeling before Jesus, stating all the good that he had done—especially his observance of the Ten Commandments, then asked Him, *"What shall I do that I may inherit eternal life?"* (Mark 10:17:1). Unfortunately, the one requirement that Jesus gave, which was to turn his whole *heart* and *life* over to God, this young man could not do. He went from wondering what he could do to be saved to seeing what he was unable to do. His abundance became his sufficiency, and like the rich will often do, he became self-reliant.

Even when our basic, physical needs are met, there is a void in our lives that *only* God can fill. Author Walter T. Connor expresses it this way: " There is something in man that will not be satisfied with the seen and the temporal. Something in him cries out for the spiritual and the eternal.

Man thirsts for God. In the midst of the visible and the transient, he reaches out after the invisible and the abiding."[23]

All men—everywhere, including all races and creeds have had some form of religion, and have cried out for God. The psalmist voices this universal cry of the human heart: *"As the hart panteth after the water brooks, so panteth my soul after thee, God"* (Psalm 42:1). Just as the life of a deer depends upon water, our lives depend upon God. We "thirst" for Him, but sometimes may feel that He isn't there; like the psalmist, we must continue to praise Him, and remember how He has blessed us before. God loves to hear our cries for Him, for then He knows that we are completely dependent upon Him. Being dependent upon the Lord is an integral part of following Him, and a small price to pay for the sacrifice that He made for us.

CHAPTER 7

"BUT THE LABOURERS ARE FEW"

"But when he saw the multitudes, he was moved with compassion on them, because they fainted, and were scattered abroad, as sheep having no shepherd. Then saith he unto his disciples, The harvest truly is plenteous, but the labourers are few; pray ye therefore the Lord of the harvest, that he will send forth labourers into his harvest" (Matthew 9:36-38).

Author Rick Warren, in his book, *The Purpose Driven Church,* states that every church has a driving force—be it tradition, personality, finances, programs, etc., as opposed to a *purpose*: "Every church is driven by something. There is a guiding force, a controlling assumption, a directing conviction behind everything that happens. It may be unspoken. It may be unknown to many. Most likely it's never been officially voted on. But it is there, influencing every aspect of the church's life."[24] Regardless of the force behind various churches, in many aspects, interests these days seems to greatly center around *activities, programs,* and especially *numbers:* number of members added to the roll; number of ministries, committees and fund-raisers; number of conferences attended/addressed, etc. But what about *souls* on the verge of being lost forever?

God is not happy when He sees sheep without a shepherd, and His anger is kindled against idle or absentee shepherds who leave their flock unattended, scattered and without knowledge (Zechariah 10:2). How many shepherds (pastors, ministers) today, serve their own concerns rather than the concerns of the people that God has entrusted to them? The position of leadership is a great responsibility, therefore, God holds these people *particularly accountable* for the spiritual condition of their flock: *"My Brethren, be not many masters, knowing that we shall receive the greater condemnation"* (James 3:1).

Leaders of the Church represent *God* and are expected to protect and preserve the sheep, not destroy them. Part of that preservation involves the overseeing of the process of discipleship. In a nutshell, leaders have the charge of monitoring the *harvest.*

Jesus makes it clear to us that around us there is always a continual *harvest.* As He looked at the crowds following Him, He had compassion on *all* the souls; even the souls of the meanest and vilest in the world are precious to the Lord of our Salvation.

Although Jesus drew large crowds, not every one who heard Him speak became His disciple—yet, to Him, they too were scattered and perishing for lack of knowledge. Today, vast multitudes are as sheep, not having a shepherd—many of whom are ready to give their lives to Christ, if *someone* will show them how. Jesus' concern was not with "numbers," but rather with souls that were empty, and waiting to be fed with the Bread of Life—they were the *harvest* He craved.

God is Lord (Husbandman) of the harvest, and it is His work to send forth labourers (John 15). Just as Jesus asked the disciples to pray for more laborers in the Kingdom that will help bring souls to Him, we, too should pray that many will be raised up and sent forth who will labor in bringing souls to Christ. Once a person is brought to Christ, however, our work is not finished. Jesus did not tell us to go and make converts—He said to go and make *disciples*. We're saturated with church buildings, members, programs, and activities. But where are the disciples—the "ambassadors for Christ?" Where are the people who, like Paul, are sold out to Christ—willing to surrender their very existence to the will of Almighty God, no matter what the price?

Our churches need men and women who first of all, know God and understand why they are on this earth—that their purpose in life is not about them, but furthering His Kingdom. "The shortage of disciples explains why we have so many Christians and so little impact within our own churches, let alone in the community at large. What we need now are not more bodies in the pews. But we desperately need more disciples. It's not how many members are in a church that matters; what counts is the number of disciples."[25]

In order to make disciples, a church must have a *vision* of the power of *multiplication*.

Before we explore the multiplicative process, let's first define the word *disciple*. A disciple is a person who has decided that following Jesus takes precedence over everything else in his or her life. Once a person becomes a disciple, he or she is ready to begin *reproducing* themselves—the multiplicative process. Paul had a clear vision as to the power of *multiplication* when he stated his goal in life: "*Whom we preach, warning every man, and teaching every man in all wisdom; that we may present every man perfect in Christ Jesus: whereunto I also labour, striving according to his working, which worketh in me mightily*" (Colossians 1:28-29).

Like Paul, we should strive to help every person we meet to mature spiritually, and we do this by affirming their potential through the power and strength of the Lord. Spiritual multiplication works like this: Each person who produces a disciple has *reproduced* himself or herself as a disciple—he has become a *worker*. When that worker has raised up a another worker, he or she has both reproduced more disciples and himself or herself as a worker. Spiritual multiplication produces both disciples and workers.

Christians are precious to God, and He has put in them a tremendous potential to develop and mature into responsible citizens in His Kingdom. This helps to explain why spiritual multiplication can never be put into a "program," rather, it must be regarded as a *ministry*. This ministry goes beyond soul-winning—it offers every believer in Jesus Christ the opportunity to achieve his or her full potential for God.

Winning a person to Christ is important; but *training* a person to win ten or one hundred people is so much more important. It's like the old adage, "Give a man a fish, and he eats for a day; teach him *how* to fish, and he eats for a lifetime." In reality, the two tasks, "winning" and "training" are combined—one is not done to the exclusion of the other, and both principles are necessary if a church is to have an effective program of evangelism. This means sticking closely to the person that we have led to Christ, then helping him or her to grow into a fruitful follower of Christ. Spending individual time with another Christian for the purpose of having a ministry in his or her life, i.e., time in the Word, prayer, training, and fellowship causes greater things to happen in one's own life.

"I've watched pastors, housewives, missionaries, nurses, building contractors, school teachers, seminary professors, and grocery owners get involved in the lives of a few people. I have seen the Lord bless their efforts and multiply their lives in Christ into the lives of others."[26]

Whenever the person that we're discipling begins to show a deep interest in helping others to grow and mature as well, another disciple is born—a *worker* and an advancement in the Kingdom of God. This is the type of worker that Jesus was talking about in our Scripture, one who is part of the *multiplicative process*. When Jesus said that the workers were few, He was talking about *harvest workers*—those who had a vision for *multiplication*. Not everyone has that particular vision, but they are just as valuable to the Kingdom in other areas, i.e., via teaching, record keeping, finances, etc.

Those workers in the Kingdom who are directly involved in the specific task of reaping souls for Christ, and then helping them *become* reapers are the *multipliers*. One of the foundational laws of the universe is *multiplication*, for everything operates on its principle: livestock, trees, flowers, even bacteria. Multiplication is just God's way of doing things. In the first commandment that God ever gave to man (and the only one that he has been able to keep), He told Adam and Eve to *"be fruitful and multiply, and replenish the earth"* (Genesis 1:28). The same explosive power that has caused man to populate the earth can be unleashed with the Gospel of Jesus Christ.

Although God wants the same principles of multiplication at work in fulfillment of the Great Commission, it becomes difficult when the population of the earth is *multiplying*, while the Church is merely *adding*. Again, Jesus was not concerned with numbers; had He been, He would never have *multiplied* His efforts through the use of disciples. Jesus didn't just bring people in to the Kingdom, without providing training for them, and neither should we.

Multiplying the Ministry

To help a man or woman go from being a convert or an untaught Christian to becoming a disciple, a worker, and then perhaps a leader, is a three step process, according to

Eims:[27] *Evangelizing; establishing; equipping; and in-depth training.*

Evangelizing: Being a witness to Jesus Christ and His work in our lives (our testimony) in obedience to His command (Mark 16:15).

Establishing: Walking with Jesus, having been firmly rooted and now being established in your faith, and overflowing with gratitude (Colossians 2:6-7).

Equipping: Working man-to-man with your disciple, leading him or her through your training objectives. The result is a *worker*—a "harvest worker"—who is now able both to evangelize, establish, and equip other workers.

In-depth Personal Training (after the pattern of Jesus): Spending concerted and quality time with the worker, taking him or her through your training objectives. The final result is a *leader* who is able to reproduce the whole process [see charts in the appendix].

"Ultimately, a leader—a servant leader is a man who can go to another pool of manpower and under the guidance of the Holy Spirit of God reproduce the kind of ministry in which he himself was raised up."[28] In the ministry of Jesus, we can see all stages of the "multiply the ministry" process. First, there was the call to repentance: *"Now that after John was put in prison, Jesus came into Galilee, preaching the gospel of the kingdom of God, and saying The time is fulfilled, and the kingdom of God is at hand: repent ye, and believe the gospel"* (Mark 1:14-15). The people who responded became *converts.*

Then Jesus issued the call to discipleship (Luke 9:23), and those who responded were disciples. He called the seventy to go out into the *harvest fields* as *workers.* Later, He called the apostles to go forth as *leaders: "Then he called his twelve disciples together, and gave them power and authority over all devils, and to cure diseases. And he sent them to preach the kingdom of God, and to heal the sick"* (Luke 9:1-2). In essence, those who responded to Jesus' call were converts, who became disciples, then workers, and finally, leaders. Training objectives for discipleship will be covered in the chapter on *nurturing*—"That These Hands Have Ministered."

The mandate to make disciples is not an option, but a command—to all who call Jesus "Lord," and we have all received gifts that will enable us, by the power of the Holy Spirit, (Acts 1:8) to fulfill the Great Commission. Whether a teacher, housewife, engineer, or minister of the faith, we are *all* called to be disciple-makers—spiritually reproducing ourselves in the lives of others. For every "Timothy" there needs to be a "Paul," nurturing and encouraging them in the *multiplicative process*. It's not enough for our churches to be open a certain number of days per week, or have a variety of programs and meetings going on; we should be making disciples—on-going!

The task of developing true, devoted, and zealous disciples has its drawbacks and obstacles, but neither methods, knowledge, time, or money are among them. In terms of knowledge, we know that the Pharisees had more religious knowledge than they had anything else. What they didn't have was the character to go with it—character that would transform them and the world around them. Judas had more than two years of exposure to the character, integrity, and teachings of Jesus, but none of it could compensate for the wickedness and treachery in his heart. So, a disciple is a person of Christian character.

The Barna Research Group, Ltd., headed by George Barna, studies discipleship in America, and has developed the Five Models of Effective Discipleship for churches to employ in their discipleship training. For the sake of space, I have chosen one of these models to discuss:

The Competencies Model

Based on the Great Commandment and the Great Commission

Broken into 30 specific competencies: *ten core beliefs, ten core practices, and ten core virtues*—all in light of one's relationship with God and other people.

10 Core Beliefs	*10 Core Practices*	*10 Core Values*
the Trinity	worship	joy
Salvation by grace	prayer	peace
authority of the Bible	single-mindedness	faithfulness
personal God	Bible study	self-control
identity in Christ	total commitment	humility
church	biblical community	love
humanity	give away your time	patience
compassion	give away your money	integrity
eternity	give away your faith	kindness
stewardship	give away your life	gentleness

The Competencies Model requires the substantive integration of everything the church does. The worship services provide inspiration to become disciples and the sermons are built around the thirty core competencies. People receive their primary theological instruction in a modified Sunday School/Adult Bible Fellowship process in which several small groups from a particular geographic area are combined into a learning community.

The groups have a trained lay pastor, and meet every Sunday morning at the church to discuss the sermon topic. Individuals then become active in ministry by belonging to a smaller group of ten to twelve people, with a trained leader.

The dominant function of the group is to be a biblical community—putting into practice the information and principles learned in the larger-group events. Areas of learning are service, evangelism, and giving. A personal spiritual evaluation tool, called a Christian Life Profile helps to evaluate each individual's virtues. The results of a person's assessment are not compared with those of other individuals, but serve as self-regulating indicators of personal strengths and weaknesses. The profile helps the individual focus on his or her spiritual condition and facilitates an appropriate domain of spiritual formation emphasis.

The competencies model does not use events, and minimizes other church programs and specialized ministries in accomplishing all ministry through the existing avenues. It would take time to sufficiently evaluate this type of model; I feel that it would be worth the effort of trying—especially since I personally "dream" of an evangelistic effort that would encompass all ministries within the church. I do not believe that evangelism has to be a separate program in the Church. I feel that it can and should be incorporated into every aspect of ministry, because saving souls and nurturing souls should be of interest and concern to every person, regardless of their position or ministry.

Other models developed by the Barna Group include: Missional Model; Neighborhood Model; Worldwide Model; and Lecture-Lab Model; none of these other models place as much weight on exposing everyone to core theological foundations as does the Competencies Model, and are shorter in content.

CHAPTER 8

"GOD HATH NOT GIVEN US THE SPIRIT OF FEAR"

Fear can be a great hindrance to the usefulness of our gifts in the Kingdom of God, especially in the realm of witnessing, for our enemy, Satan, has positioned many barriers that has kept many Christians from telling others about Christ and His free gift of Salvation and eternal life. But praise be to our omniscient, omnipotent, omnipresent, and awesome God, who has delivered us from the spirit of fear and replaced it with a spirit of courage and resolution, we can learn to share our faith with *confidence*: *"Wherefore I put thee in remembrance that thou stir up the gift of God, which is in thee by the putting on of my hands. For God hath not given us the spirit of fear; but of power, and of love, and of a sound mind"* (2 Timothy 1:6-7).

All Christians know that they should witness for Christ (Acts 1:8), but many put off doing it as long as possible, until the "guilt" gets too great for him or her to bear; then they're likely to overpower the next non-Christian they meet with a rehearsed, non-stop monologue. Others just don't bother to witness at all. In both instances, they have bought into one or more of the enemy's lies: "People will think that you're a religious fanatic," "Your religion is personal and private," "You might offend someone," "You'll only start an argument," "Witnessing is for missionaries or evangelists—like Billy Graham." Satan *is* our enemy (2 Corinthians 4:4; James 4:7; 1 Peter 5:8), and his methods are deceitful (Ephesians 6:11-12).

Satan in not omniscient, but he knows our defects and vulnerability. After the fall of man, every human became a member of Satan's dark and gloomy kingdom; non-believers are still there, either by choice, ignorance or default. Satan resents the fact that God has liberated Christians from his "prison," and is doing everything he can to prevent anyone else from receiving the Good News, and thus, being liberated. As you and I sense God leading us to witness to someone, Satan also senses it and dispatches his agents to the scene. His scheme is to make us think twice, turn back, and abandon our mission. Any level of *fear* that the enemy can orchestrate, he will!

For instance, you're about to seize an opportunity to witness to someone. The enemy may try to make you feel as if you'd be "forcing" your religion on someone else; or he may tell you to "mind our own business," or that it is *none* of your business. Any instant whereby someone needs to hear about Christ Jesus and His free gift of Salvation is absolutely, positively, unequivocally your business! It is business that you've been *commanded* to do (Matthew 28:19-20), e*mpowered* to do (Acts 1:8), and *entrusted* to do (1 Corinthians 9:19-23), and hence, must not allow *fear* of any kind to sabotage your witness.

Fear of being told "no" can lead to feelings of embarrassment, as none of us rejoices at the thought of being "turned down," but fear *of failure* is one of the largest cripplers of a faithful witness. Guess "who" is behind both?! We suffer these feelings of rejection and failure because the

Enemy works hard at trying to convince us that *we're* responsible for the *results* of witnessing—and we're *not*—God is! Saving souls is His work—not ours. In His Word, He doesn't say to us, "Go, and save people," rather, "Go, and teach..." Our job is to "plant," and leave the harvesting to the Lord.

Sure, it's hurting when you've reached out in genuine love to someone, and they've refused the greatest Gift God could ever offer to mankind—His precious, only begotten Son (John 3:16). Tears and heartache are a reality in the sphere of compassion for the lost. Even Jesus, who *is* the Redeemer, did not grieve from a bruised ego; He grieved because people had rejected the Giver of life and the Gift of *eternal* life. In spite of rejection and what some may deem as "failures," Jesus could take comfort and peace in knowing that He had obeyed the command of His Father.

As Jesus neared the completion of His mission, He lifted up His eyes to heaven, and ended His prayer for the cause of evangelism: *I have glorified thee on earth: I have finished the work which thou gavest me to do. And, now, O Father, glorify thou me with thine own self with the glory which I had with thee before the world was"* (John 17:4-5).

There is nothing comparable to being able to say, with confidence, that one has been faithful to his or her call.

Like Jesus, Paul could face his own death calmly—knowing that he had been faithful in his calling: *"I have fought a good fight, I have finished my course, I have kept the faith: henceforth there is a crown of righteousness, which the Lord, the righteous judge, shall give me at that day: and not to me only, but unto all them also that love his appearing"* (2 Timothy 4:7).

Paul is telling us that no matter how difficult the fight seems—keep fighting, because the "crown" will be for all those who endured until the end. What Christian, at the end of his or her journey, wouldn't want to hear the Lord say,

"Well done, thou good and faithful servant: thou hast been faithful over a few things, I will make thee ruler over many things: enter thou into the joy of the Lord" (Matthew 25:21).

Enduring until the end encompasses two other "barriers" that prevent some Christians from witnessing: Lack of training (practical "know-how"), and lethargy.[29] In dealing with the latter, a close look at Paul's words to the Christian community at Rome shows his concern for their spiritual lethargy. Perhaps Paul was speaking to the "spiritually lazy" and biblically illiterate of the Church: *"And do not conform to the present world system but by the renewal of your mind, so as to sense for yourselves what is the good and acceptable and perfect will of God"* (Romans 12:2).

Rightfully so, we usually associate this verse with repentance and right behavior; but it goes deeper than the level of behavior—it is an admonition to *know for one's self*—to not only renew, but *reeducate* and *redirect* our minds. Were the Christian Romans, like too many of us in the Church are today—satisfied with someone else "knowing for us," having no desire to know for ourselves? Are we spoon-fed Christians, desiring "comfortable Christianity?" Is wrestling with truth so time consuming that we prefer that biblical truth and God-wisdom be ground up or pureed for us?

Ultimately, we want the pastor to tell us how to live in a particular situation—without studying the guidelines formulated by God Himself. God never intended for His sons and daughters to rely on "prescriptive faith."

> It is a dangerous posture to entrust the information concerning our salvation into the hands of someone else. Mature faith requires that one engage in the struggle of searching for God's will in every situation. Responsible Christian faith calls us to be responsible to enjoin the presence of God in the

unfolding roads and plains of the human struggle. We cannot do this with inadequate information.[30]

Sound teaching is at the core of any healthy evangelism effort, as it was one of three methods used by our Lord Jesus in attracting and holding crowds. Jesus loved people, met their needs, and *taught* them. Scripture tells us that the crowds were: amazed at His teaching: *"the people were astonished at his doctrine"* (Matthew 7:28) and profoundly impressed *"and when the multitude heard this, they were astonished at his doctrine* (22:33; Mark 11:18); and *enjoyed* listening to him (12:37).

If we want to capture the attention of unbelievers as Jesus did, we must communicate spiritual truth the way He did. But first we have to know *truth,* ourselves, and *how* to communicate it to non-believers. Therefore, Church members should be "learning people," as were the believers in the early Church, who devoted themselves to the apostles' teaching: *"and they continued steadfastly in the apostles' doctrine...."* (Acts 2:42).

It has been said that, "when we cease to learn, we cease to live," for *"Thy Word is a Lamp unto our feet, and a Light unto our path"* (Psalm 119:105), and *"Faith cometh by hearing, and hearing by the word of God"* (Romans 10:17). But Gods Word must be hidden in our hearts, and practiced in our lives, in order to effectively lead people to Christ.[31] Several authors of books on evangelism give helpful outlines for successful evangelism: (a) various *stages of sharing Jesus*; (b) different *steps* in leading a person to Christ; and (c) numerous ways of *leading a conversation* to Christ.

Darrell Robinson, in his book, *People Sharing Jesus*, describes four stages to be recognized in the laws or principles of sowing and reaping that apply to sharing Jesus:

1. The Soil-Preparation Stage
2. The Sowing Stage
3. The Cultivation Stage
4. The Harvest Stage

In the *soil-preparation stage,* the "soil" of the non-believer must be "prepared" to receive the seed of the Gospel; God does this through spiritual awakening, and it must begin with us—the believers: *"For the time is come that judgment must begin at the house of God: and if it first begin at us, what shall the end be of them that obey not the gospel of God? And if the righteous scarcely be saved, where shall the ungodly and the sinner appear?"* (1 Peter 4:17-18). God's people are being *called* to Him as never before.

We must confess our sins, repent, and yield to Christ, before we can expect to permeate a community, to reach others. Spirit-filled, Christ-centered lives of believers affirm the presence and power of God. When the Holy Spirit came at Pentecost, the lives of Christ's followers impacted the world around them, *"And the Lord added to the church daily such as should be saved"* (Acts 2:47). Just as a farmer breaks up the hard surface soil of his field—to soften it and rid it of weeds, God will "break up" the unplowed ground in the hearts of non-believers, to prepare the soil for the seed of His Word. He has promised to "heal" our land: *"If my people, who are called by my name, will humble themselves, and pray, and seek my face, and turn from their wicked ways, then will I hear from heaven and will forgive their sin and will heal their land"* (2 Chronicles 7:14).

God is telling us, as He told His people in Jeremiah's day, to break up the hardness of their hearts: *"Break up your fallow ground, and sow not among thorns. Circumcise yourselves to the Lord, and take away the foreskins of your heart...lest my fury come forth like fire, and burn that none can quench it, because of the evil of your doings"* (4:3). God wants to use us to prepare unbelieving ground for the *sowing* of His Word.

As the witnessing believer does his *sowing,* he or she has an advantage over the farmer who sows seeds, in that a harvest can be gathered as the seed of the Gospel is being sown.

In such instance, someone else has previously done the sowing. Jesus states it this way: *"And he that reapeth receiveth wages, and gathereth fruit unto life eternal: that both he that soweth and he that reapeth may rejoice together. And herein is that saying true, One soweth, and another reapeth"* (John 4:36-37). For a continuous harvest, sowing of seed (sharing Jesus) must be continual and consistent. Commitment is essential, for our Enemy, Satan, will do everything he can to block our witnessing.

In the *cultivation stage*, believers are the "instruments," for the Holy Spirit does the cultivating. As we witness, He works to cultivate the hearts of those that do not know Him, working through all types of circumstances in their lives, i.e., disappointment, illness, death, guilt, blessings and successes. The key is that the Holy Spirit makes people *realize* the need for God in their lives. No doubt, the woman at the well was disappointed and had given up on marriage, for she was living with a man who was not her husband. Her need was forgiveness and a new start. The Holy Spirit drew her to the Living Water, which changed her life.

A time of illness will open the door to the *harvest,* and for the Holy Spirit to draw the sick to the Great Physician for healing, such as the woman with the "issue of blood" (Mark 5:25-34). The Lord works through death (Jairus' daughter, vv35-43), and even guilt in one's life. The Holy Spirit has *convicting power* that can make even the unsaved vulnerable to it; through the heaviness of his own guilt, a conscious-stricken Saul of Tarsus became open to Jesus by way of his vulnerability to the Holy Spirit. When confronted with the risen Christ, all Saul could say was, *"Lord, what wilt thou have me to do?"* (Acts 9:6).

The Lord Himself is the Owner of the *harvest,* and we, as Christians go (with His authority) into the harvest to witness. Per the *harvest stage*, we must keep in mind that few of the unsaved will come to the churches to be reached. So, in order to reach the them, we must go where they are—as Jesus did. *"And he went about all the cities and villages, teaching in their synagogues, and preaching the gospel of the kingdom, and healing every sickness and every disease among the people"* (Matthew 9:35). Jesus didn't overlook anyone, and we can't afford to either. He went to the large cities, small villages, and even the open country side, battling three deadly enemies of evangelism: sin, ignorance, and disease.

To combat the enemy of sin, Jesus preached the Kingdom of God and His righteousness; He taught the truth to overcome ignorance; and for the enemy of disease, He healed. Today, we live in the midst of hurting, devastated, hopeless people also; as Christians, we are all shepherds, who must equip ourselves to share Jesus with them, and to give them the spiritual nurture and support they need. As ambassadors for Christ, we all battle the same Enemy as did Jesus and all the other evangelists; therefore we must *pray*, as Jesus did, that the Holy Spirit will convict the nonbeliever, and give him or her a strong desire for the ways of God. One thing we must remember, however, is that God's sovereign timing is different from ours, despite our intensive prayers.

We still know that *God is not willing that anyone perish"* (2 Peter 3:9), but until *He* works in the heart of a person, nothing is going to happen. Why must we continue to witness, even if we do not see the immediate results? Jesus gives a perfect illustration in His parable of the Sower:

"A farmer was sowing grain in his fields. As he scattered the seed across the ground, some fell beside a path, and the birds came and ate it. And some fell on rocky soil where there was little depth of earth; the plants sprang up quickly enough in the shallow soil, but the hot sun soon scorched them and they withered and died, for they had so little root. Other seeds fell among thorns, and the thorns choked out the tender blades. But some fell on good soil, and produced a crop that was thirty, sixty, and even a hundred times as much as he had planted" (Matthew 13:3-8, TLB).

The four types of soil represent different responses to Christ's message; people respond differently because each person is in a different state of "readiness." Christ is teaching that out of the four types of listeners in the harvest, only one of the four types will take the message and put it to work in his or her life. He said that, while the good ground represents the heart of a man who listens to the message and understands it and goes out and brings thirty, sixty, and even a hundred others into the Kingdom (v. 23, TLB), the other three listeners (types of soil) will either squander the message or reject it outright.

Man is in a position to exercise his *God-given power of free choice* both for and against God. Although the "no's" will come, we must always pre-suppose a positive response, because God can take what we might consider a failure and use it to bring that sister or brother to Him. We must continue to plant positive seeds in people's lives, and trust God to bring forth the fruit.

CHAPTER 9

"THAT THESE HANDS HAVE MINISTERED"

―――

"For I have not shunned to declare unto you all the counsel of God. Take heed therefore unto yourselves, and to all the flock... the Holy Ghost hast made you overseers....Ye yourselves know, that these hands have ministered unto my necessities, and to them that were with me. I have shewed you all things" (Acts 20:27-35).

In Paul's farewell discourse to the elders at Ephesus, he wasn't just saying good-bye to a few friends—he was leaving a legacy to the people who, for years, he had *given himself away* to. People he had loved, cared for, prayed for, even cried over—the epitome of what *nurturing* is all about. The lives of the people he touched were important to Paul, no matter where he went, and regardless of his circumstances. He didn't just plant a church, or preach to people— he *nurtured them,* sometimes, if only by letter. In fact, Paul would send a follow-up letter to each of the churches that he visited, encouraging them to continue in their faith, and letting them know that he was praying for them. Now that he was leaving for Jerusalem, never to see their faces again, Paul is telling these people whom he nurtured—as well as all Christians, to follow his example—"nourish your flocks."

Our "flocks" are not confined to church pews, for we are *all* ministers of the faith (Romans 12:7), responsible for leading souls to the lordship of Jesus Christ. But once we lead a soul to Christ, then what? New "babes in Christ" are brand-new to the Kingdom, and are just beginning their spiritual lives; they have the same needs as they had as new born babies: *food, love, acceptance, and protection— nurturing.*

The care and protection of the *spiritual infant*— spiritual pediatrics[32] deals with the development of new babes in Christ, from the time of their new birth (John 3:3), until they grow and provide for themselves. Just as we're appalled at the news of a baby being abandoned or neglected, we should also grieve at the thought of a new babe in Christ being forsaken; left alone, a new babe in Christ either slips into carnality or he or she will never grow in grace and the knowledge of our Lord and Savior Jesus Christ.

Assurance

The first need a convert has is *assurance*—he needs to know that he or she has been born again.[33] The one who is discipling him or her needs to know that too. A person may make the decision to accept Christ, but remain dead in his trespasses and sin. As one man, who had been baptized three times put it, "twice, I went down (in the water) a 'dry sinner', and I emerged a 'wet sinner.' The third time, however, I really had *changed,* both in attitude and life style. Now my baptism has meaning for me."

Paul told the Corinthians that if anyone is in Christ, he's a *new creation*—the old person is *gone*, and a new one has come! (2 Corinthians 5:17); to the Colossians, he expressed it this way: *"As ye have therefore received Christ Jesus the*

Lord, so walk ye in him: rooted and built up in him, and stablished in the faith, as ye have been taught" (2:6-7a). New Christians aren't expected to fully understand the doctrine of the lordship of Jesus Christ over their lives — nor are all their problems solved. But they are brand-new people on the *inside*, so we should certainly see a change of attitude toward Christ, and a change of attitude toward *sin*. Confession of sin and cleansing is part of the conversion experience: *"If we confess our sins, he is faithful and just to forgive us our sins, and to cleanse us from all unrighteousness"* (1 John 1:9).

Love and Acceptance

The convert needs to know that, in admitting his or her sins, he or she is *agreeing* with God concerning the sin, and are *willing to turn* from it. It is at this point that the convert needs to know that he or she is *loved and accepted*, in spite of the sin confessed: *"If any man sin, we have an advocate with the Father, Jesus Christ the righteous: and he is the propitiation for our sins..."* (2:1-2). The love and assurance that Paul gave to the Thessalonians made them powerful in their Christian lives and testimonies (1 Thessalonians 1:7-8).

The new convert needs to feel free to share his or her doubts, fears, anxieties, or personal problems, without feeling condemned or rejected because of them. Peter taught that charity (love) covers all sins or infractions: *"And above all things have fervent charity among yourselves: for charity shall cover the multitude of sins. Use hospitality one to another without grudging"* (1 Peter 4:8).

Protection

Because a new babe in Christ will be "prime" prey for false teachers (cults) and also for attacks from the enemy, they need our protection. When old "cronies" show up to try to entice the convert back to the old paths of destruction, he or she needs to know how to resist the temptation, yet remain a good example in the presence of the unsaved. One of the more commonly used tactics is to remind the convert of their past deeds: "Since when did you become so holy? I remember when you did...!" Christ's example is the best one to present to the new Christian, for He never answered back when He was insulted, and never threatened to "get even; He left His case in the hands of God—who always judges fairly.

Paul told the Corinthians to be separate from unbelievers: *"Wherefore come out from among them, and be separate, saith the Lord, and touch not the unclean thing"* (2 Corinthians 6:17). This Scripture is not just telling us to keep our distance from sinners, but also to stay close to God. It is impossible to daily avoid all influences of sin, for sin is everywhere. The media capitalizes on it, the entertainment world is influenced by it, and merchants set their marketing efforts by its appeal to the public. As the new babe in Christ matures, he or she will learn that Christians are still expected to witness to unbelievers. Jesus dined in the homes of sinners, even went out of His way to have an encounter with them, for the sake of witnessing.

"Satan regroups and marshals his counteroffensive, and the new Christian is particularly vulnerable because he does not understand the nature of spiritual warfare or the great truths in the Bible that can help him through trials and temptation."[34] One of Satan's notorious deceptions is to make the new Christian believe that the problems or trials he or she is experiencing are *unique* to him or her. We need to let new converts know that we all fight the same Enemy and his forces: *"For we wrestle not against flesh and blood, but against principalities, against powers, against the rulers of the darkness of this world, against spiritual wickedness in high places"* (Ephesians 6:12). It helps also, if the new Christians know that we will stand with them against these forces.

Paul gave strong encouragement to the Corinthians regarding temptation, and God's help for us in resisting it: *"There hath no temptation taken you but such as common to man: but God is faithful, who will not suffer you to be tempted above that ye are able; but will with the temptation also make a way to escape, that ye may be able to bear it"* (1 Corinthians 10:13). When it comes to temptation, none of us is singled out—it happens to everyone. With the help of God, any temptation can be resisted. We must help the new convert to understand: how to recognize people and situations that give them trouble; to run from anything they know is wrong; there is no right way to do a wrong thing; pray for God's help; and seek friends and acquaintances who love God and can offer help in overcoming.

Fellowship

The new Christian has been "born" into the family of God, and therefore needs the *fellowship* of his brothers and sisters in Christ. The way for new believers to grow and mature in their faith is to be with other believers where they can learn God's Word, pray, and share. The new Christians of the first church were joined with other believers, were taught by the apostles, and included in prayer meetings and fellowship: *"And all that believed were together, and had all things in common...continuing daily with one accord in the temple, and breaking bread from house to house...praising God, and having favour with all the people"* (Acts 2:44-47).

Spiritual Food

Just as natural babies are fed with regularity, so Spiritual babies must be *fed* regularly, and the Word of God is the spiritual food. But we don't keep spoon-feeding them, or keep them on the spiritual "milk bottle." We are to teach them to feed themselves—to "dig" and search on their own; otherwise, they will be dependent upon others—never growing and developing into strong disciples for Christ, or able to "multiply" themselves.

Prayer

Another vital part of spiritual nourishment is quiet time with God, each day. The new Christian needs a consistent quiet time—a time to be away from others and talk with God, even if he or she has to get up before daybreak to do it: *"And in the morning, rising up a great while before day, he went out, and departed into a solitary place, and there prayed"* (Mark 1:35). If our Lord and Savior Jesus Christ needed time and prayer with His Father, to start His day, certainly every Christian should follow suit.

Prayer has always had a large place in the lives of God's people. When Abraham prayed for the wicked city of Sodom, he was well aware of the fact that God is just, and that He punishes sin. Yet, he prayed for God's *mercy* on these people (Genesis 18:20-33). When He spared the city, God proved to Abraham that asking for anything is allowed—with the understanding that His answers come from His own perspective. There are many other Scriptures that can teach the new Christian that there is nothing too hard for God: Psalm 90 (Moses); 1 Kings 18:36 (Elijah); Psalm 72:20 (David) Romans 1:9 (Paul).

Other areas that can help a new Christian in the area of prayer are:

Why We Should Pray
1. To worship and praise God: John 4:23-24; Romans 15:11; Hebrews 13:15
2. To receive things of God: John 16:24; James 4:2
3. To strengthen our spiritual nature: 1 John 3:9; John 15:11; 17:13
4. It is *commanded*: 1 Thessalonians 5:17; Luke 18:1; Philippians 4:6; 1 Timothy 2:8.

How We Should Pray
1. Addressing our prayer to the Father: Matthew 6:9; John 16:26-27
2. Depending upon the aid of the Holy Spirit: Romans 8:26-27; John 14:16
3. Trusting the intercession of our High Priest, Jesus Christ: Hebrews 4:14-16.
4. In the *will of God*: John 14:13-14; 1 John 5:14-15.
5. With all sin confessed and forsaken: Psalm 51; 66:18
6. In simple, resting faith: Mark 11:24
7. Unselfishly: James 4:2-3
8. With God's glory being the overall entity: Psalm 79:9; 2 Chronicles 14:11; Jeremiah 14:7.

When and Where We Should Pray
1. Any place, at any time: Luke 18:1; Romans 12:12; Colossians 4:2.
2. At regular, stated times: Matthew 6:6 (private devotions); Genesis 17:18; Matthew 15:22; Philemon 2 (Family altar); Acts 4:23-24 (public meetings).
3. Necessary in struggling with hindering forces: Jeremiah 29:7; Matthew 5:44.
4. For others (intercessory): 1 Timothy 2:1; James 5:14, 16; Psalm 122:6; Isaiah 62:6-7.

To help the new convert get started in time of prayer, the following acrostic ACTS may be helpful:

Adoration: Worship and prayer over the greatness of God.
Confession: Acknowledging our sinfulness and dependence upon the Lord.
Thanksgiving: Enumerating the many blessings bestowed upon us by God.
Supplication: Petitioning (personal) and intercession (on behalf of others).

Bible Reading:

The more we seek God, the more He will reveal to us. Once a new babe in Christ sees his or her need for God's Word, and begin to find nourishment in Christ, the spiritual appetite increases and they begin to mature: *"As newborn babes, desire the sincere milk of the word, that ye may grow thereby: if so be ye have tasted that the Lord is gracious"* (1 Peter 2:2). Many books, pamphlets, and quarterly booklets, such as *Our Daily Bread, The Upper Room,* etc., are refreshing and inspiring to "seasoned" Christians, and certainly can be quite helpful to new Christians. They also make excellent gifts for a disciple to give his or her new convert. In my *discipleship*, this type of giving has been an additional ministry in and of itself.

Bible Study

The new convert needs to be exposed to mature Christians who can not only feed and teach them the "whole counsel of God," but also work closely with them, encouraging them to stay with it. In terms of Bible-study aids, the new babes in Christ need the kind that will teach them how to feed themselves. It would be helpful for the disciple to prepare a lesson with the new Christian. The Bible is the textbook of Christian doctrine, and the instrument for Christian service; it is the *seed of the sower:* 1 Peter 1:23-25; it is the *sword of the soldiers*: Ephesians 6:17; and it is the *sermon of the speaker:* Romans 10:8.

The Work of a Christian

Works do not save us, but saved people work! "We are saved to serve." The Bible has much to say about works: **We are saved *from* works** - Hebrews 6:1; 9:14; Romans 10:1-3; Ephesians 2:1-3. **We are saved *without* works** - Ephesians 2:8-9; Titus 3:3-7. **We are saved *unto* works** - Titus 3:1; 8, 14; Ephesians 2:8-10. We are saved unto good works, in which God has prearranged that we should spend our lives. For examples, read Isaiah 6:9-11; Jeremiah 1:4-10, 17-19; Ezekiel 2:3-3:12; and Acts 9:12-16.

In other words, God has a plan for each of our lives. We are here for His purpose, not ours. Our prayer should be to align our purpose with His purpose, and our will with His will for our lives.

Salvation

The new babe in Christ should have a *clear* understanding of what the Scriptures teach on the *plan of Salvation*:

Romans 3:23............................Everyone has sinned: *"For all have sinned and come short of the glory of God."*

Romans 6:23............................The penalty for our sin is death: *"For the wages of sin is death; but the gift of God is eternal life."*

Romans 5:8................................Jesus Christ died for sin: *"But God commendeth His love toward us, in that, while we were yet sinners, Christ died for us."*

Romans 10:9-10............................To be forgiven for our sin, we must believe and confess that Jesus is Lord. Salvation comes through Jesus Christ: *"If thou shalt confess with thy mouth the Lord Jesus, and shalt believe in thine heart that God hath raised him from the dead, thou shalt be saved."*

John 3:16...........................God loves us: *"For God so loved the world, that he have his only begotten Son, that whosoever believeth in Him* *should not perish, but have everlasting life."*

Ephesians 2:8-9..............We can do absolutely nothing to save ourselves: *"For by grace are ye saved through faith: And that not or yourselves: It is the gift of God: Not of works, lest any man should boast."*

Christian Ordinances

Although Baptism and The Lord's Supper is observed differently among the varied denominations and churches, the basis and meaning of these two sacred ordinances are clearly substantiated by Scripture:

Baptism

Symbol:
  (1) The death, burial and resurrection of Christ: Romans 6:4-5.
  (2) The Believer's identity with Christ in His death, burial, and resurrection, together with Him: 2 Corinthians 5:14-21.
  (3) The Believer's death to the old life, and resurrection to the new: Colossians 2:12; 2 Corinthians 5:17.

Mode:
  (1) It is a burial: Romans 6:4-5.
  (2) The literal meaning of the Greek word translated "baptize," is to "dip" or "immerse." Bible accounts carried this out: The Lord Jesus came "up out of the water." Matthew 3:16. John was baptizing at Jordan because "there was much water there." John 3:23.

Candidates for Baptism:
  (1) Those who have repented of their sins: Acts 2:38.

(2) Those who receive Jesus Christ by faith as Saviour and Lord: Acts 2:36, 41; 8:36-37; 18:8.

Holy Communion

Significance:
Symbolizes the atoning death of Christ: 1 Corinthians 11:26.
Symbolizes our spiritual nourishment: Matthew 26:26-27.
It is a memorial of the death of Christ: Luke 22:19.
It is a type of our fellowship (communion) with the Lord Jesus: 1 Corinthians 10:16-17.
It is a prophecy of the "Marriage Supper of the Lamb." Matthew 26:29; Revelation 19:7-9.

Authority:
The example and command of Christ: Matthew 26:26-30.
A special revelation to Paul: 1 Corinthians 11:23-29.
The practice of the Apostolic Church: Acts 2:41-42; 1 Corinthians 10:16.

Qualifications:
Conversion: Acts 2:41-42.
A godly life, all known sins confessed and forsaken: 1 Corinthians 11:27-32; 1 John 1:9.
*The Lord's Supper stands between Christ's first coming (Advent) and His return (Second Coming), pointing to each—it speaks of faith in His finished work on Calvary and hope of His coming again.

The Grace of Giving—Stewardship

While much controversy may exist in many denominations and churches, in regards to the interpretation of giving, tithing, and stewardship, there are certain truths in God's holy and righteous Word that cannot be denied:

God is Owner of All Things (Psalm 50:10-12), and He owns by three rights:
1. He is Creator - Genesis 1:1; John 1:1-3.
2. His priority–He was before all things: Psalm 90:2.
3. His Supremacy: Psalm 10:16; 47:2, 7-10.
4. He has never relinquished that right: Genesis 2:15-17; 9:1-7; Leviticus 17:11; 25:23; Genesis 17:5-8.

As Christians We Belong To God:
1. By natural creation: Job 33:4.
2. By re-creation, or New Birth: 2 Corinthians 5:17.
3. By redemption: 1 Corinthians 6:19-20.

God Has Made Provision For Us to Acknowledge His Ownership:
1. By returning a tenth of our increase to Him: Leviticus 27:30; 1 Corinthians 9:12-14; Matthew 23:23; 1 Corinthians 16:1-2-.
2. Free-will offerings above the tenth: 2 Corinthians 9:6-7.
3. Blessings for those who honor God in giving: Proverb 3:9-10; Malachi 3:8-10.
4. Giving God the "high-five."

As a summation of our stewardship requirements, the "high-five" that we must give God says it all: 1) *our time;* 2) *our treasure;* 3) *our talent;* 4) *our testimony, and* 5) *our temple.* We are to make the most of our *time* in regards to worship, work, family, and even resting (Ephesians 5:16). With our *talent,* we're expected to help the entire Church with our gifts and abilities (1 Corinthians 12:7). In regard to our *testimony,* we're instructed to always be ready to give answers, when asked, concerning our faith and hope (1 Peter 3:15).

It has been said that if you want to know a person's sentiments and commitment concerning God, look at his or her checkbook! The Lord says that the way we regard and use our *treasure* is indicative of where our heart is (Matthew 6:19-24). It comes as news to some that our bodies are not our own, and that the way we treat our *temple* is an indicator of who "owns" it. If God owns it, we will not violate His standards for living in it. *"What? Know ye not that your body is the temple of the Holy Ghost which is in you, which ye have of God, and ye are not your own?"* (1 Corinthians 6:19).

We were *"bought with a price: therefore glorify God in your body, and in your spirit, which are God's"* (v. 20). Besides teaching new Christians, being a good example is one of the best ways to teach another person. Paul told the Philippians to put into practice whatever they had learned from him: *"Those things, which ye have both learned and received, and heard, and seen in me, do"* (4:9). We know the consequences of violating the rules in a building that we rent; by the same token, because our souls reside in a "building" owned by Someone else (God), we must adhere to His code of ethics. Our Father is holy, and He expects holy living from His children.

CHAPTER 10

"AS EVERY MAN HATH RECEIVED THE GIFT"

―❦―

"As every man hath received the gift, even so minister the same one to another, as good stewards of the manifold grace of God....if any man minister, let him do it as of the ability which God giveth: that God in all things may be glorified through Jesus Christ, to whom be praise and dominion for ever and ever. Amen" (1 Peter 4:10-11).

Contrary to the plan of God, there are churches where it seems as if the pastor is doing all the work, and "it is well with the soul" of the congregation—after all, isn't that what he or she is getting paid for? In this scenario, there is no growth, neither on the part of the members, nor on the part of the church, because the *spiritual gifts* of the members are not being developed or utilized. Pastors should never try to, or be expected, to do everything in the church. Rather, the work of the church should be spread out among its members: *"It is not reason that we should leave the word of God, and serve tables. Wherefore, brethren, look ye out among you.....whom we may appoint over this business. But we will give ourselves continually to prayer, and to the ministry of the word"* (Acts 2a-4).

Jethro gave Moses, his son-in-law the most wise and sound advice that can be heeded by any pastor—"you can't do it alone!" (Exodus 18:13-26). He told him that, trying to do everything would wear him (Moses) out as well as the people. Spiritually mature, and wise men and women are capable of leading our churches, and each member in the church has been given special gifts to be used to build up and edify the Kingdom of God.

Unfortunately, many members of the Church fall short in actually using their spiritual gifts, either because they are *unaware* of their gifts, or of their commission to serve. We are *saved to serve*: *"But now we are delivered from the law, that being dead wherein we were held; that we should serve in newness of spirit"* (Romans 7:6). Newness of spirit means that Jesus frees us to serve Him out of love and gratitude, as the *fruit* of the Spirit (Galatians 5:22) is being produced in us. God never asks us to do something we cannot do, or perform a task without first *equipping* us for it. He may ask a person to do something *he* may not think he can do.

Moses felt that he was not the man to represent God before Pharaoh and the people of Egypt; but God assured him that he was the right man, and that *He* would endow him with the necessary gifts to accomplish the task. God both calls and equips, and the equipment is called "gifts." Some people may need clarification as to what the Bible refers to as *gifts*.

Our gifts are the *manifold grace of God*, and are to be used for *serving others*, not for our own exclusive enjoyment. Thus, every time we use our gifts in that manner, we are ministering God's *grace* to others. J. E. O' Day defines a spiritual gift as " God's enabling power made visible by means of a particular type of activity which serves other people."[35]

Since grace is the source of our gifts, and each of us is different, it stands to reason that our gifts would correspond to the particular grace we have received: *"Having then gifts differing according to the grace that is given to us, whether prophecy, let us prophecy according....or ministry, let us wait on our ministering: or on teaching...he that giveth...he that ruleth...he that sheweth mercy"* (Romans 12:6-8).

Spiritual gifts differ in nature, power, wisdom, and effectiveness, according to God's wisdom and graciousness—not according to one's faith. Following is a description of specific spiritual gifts listed in the Bible, and their relationship to the will of God:

The Prophet: One with the Spirit-given capacity and desire to serve God by proclaiming God's truth. Prophecy is not always a prediction about the future, but often means preaching God's messages; the hell-fire-brimstone preacher who points out sin. Prophets are often bold and articulate.

The Evangelist: One with the Spirit-given capacity and desire to serve God by leading people to the saving knowledge of Jesus Christ. The bold, aggressive soul-winner who seeks the lost.

The Teacher: One with the Spirit-given capacity and desire to serve God by making clear the truth of the Word of God, with accuracy and simplicity. The scholar making clear the doctrines and teachings of the Bible. Teachers are clear thinkers.

The Exhorter: One with the Spirit-given capacity and desire to serve God by motivating others to action by urging them to pursue a course of conduct. A "how-to" teacher, giving the application of God's Word. A preacher of the Word.

The Pastor/Teacher: One with the Spirit-given capacity and desire to serve God by assuming the responsibility for the spiritual welfare of a group of Christians: overseeing, training, and caring for the needs of a congregation.

The shepherd who *leads and feeds.*

The Administrator: One with the Spirit-given capacity and desire to serve God by leading the church and its ministries: organizing, administering, leading, managing and promoting the various affairs of the church.

The Mercy-Shower: One with the Spirit-given capacity and desire to serve God by feeling empathy and compassion for those in distress. The person who identifies with and comforts fellow Christians.

The Server: One with the Spirit-given capacity and desire to serve God by rendering practical help in both spiritual and physical matters. One who can identify unmet needs and use available resources therein.

The Giver: One with the Spirit-given capacity and desire to serve God by contributing their material resources, including and far beyond the tithe, to further the work of the Kingdom. This person is also willing to meet the financial needs of fellow Christians.

The biblical list of gifts do not claim to be exhaustive, for the Bible does not claim that the gifts listed by the apostles are the only ones that God has given to His children. There are many other functions and services within the Church that one may be capable of rendering, but are not listed in Scripture. Even abilities that a person may have had as a non-Christian can be used by God to further His work. We should always remember that Jesus' disciples had shortcomings, but they were still useful to the Kingdom. Jesus used Peter's "big mouth" and spontaneity at Pentecost to start His Church!

Any talents or abilities that we have are God-given, and become spiritual when they are controlled and energized by the Holy Spirit, and we each have a specific place in the Body of Christ (the Church). In helping a disciple to discover his or her gift, we need to get them involved with other members of the Body. Giving themselves to others will help bring their own gifts to light. Noticing where their interests lie, and where they seem to exercise faith is also helpful in discovering their gifts.

O'day has an interesting method of experimentation in discovering spiritual gifts: "Put it to work and see (1) if you enjoy using this gift, (2) if other people benefit from your use of this gift, and (3) if you feel comfortable and fulfilled exercising it. In brief, find out if this gift fits you. If it stems from the grace that God has given your unique self, then it will fit—it will correspond to the new you God has made."[36]

The disciple needs to know early on what his or her gifts are, and once discovered, it's time to develop and use them for God's Kingdom. Our gifts must be in *harmony* with our calling. Also, we must accept responsibility in the area of our gift, then take an inventory of the opportunities available in our church and community for using our gifts. The one thing we must remember, and caution our new disciples is *spiritual pride* or *jealousy*.

As members of God's family, we have different gifts, but we are united by one Spirit into one spiritual Body. Instead of comparing ourselves to one another, we are to use our different gifts, together, to proclaim the Good News.

Paul used the analogy of the human body to emphasize the importance of each member of the Body of Christ. *"For as the body is one; and hath many members, and all the members of that one body, being many, are one body: so also is Christ. For by one Spirit are we all baptized into one body... God hath tempered the body together...that there should be no schism in the body*; but that the members should have the same care one for another" (1 Corinthians 12:12-25).

Spiritual Gifts and Evangelism:

Evangelism itself is not a spiritual gift, but the loving responsibility of every born-again Christian. It is explaining to people what it means to be a Christian and to become one, according to the Scriptures: *"And working together with Him, we also urge you not to receive the grace of God in vain—for He says, At the acceptable time I listened to you, and on the day of salvation I helped you; behold, now is the acceptable time, behold, now is The day of salvation."* (2 Corinthians 6:1-2).

The *gift of evangelism* is not preaching the Gospel, it is *motivating, training, and equipping* Christians to do the work of evangelism: *"And he gave some evangelists....for the equipping of the saints for the work of service, to the building up of the body of Christ"* (Ephesians 4:11-12). An *evangelist* is a Christian God has called to full time evangelism work, with the primary job of reaping fruit of the harvest of born-again Christians doing evangelism work with their free time: *"Say not ye, there are yet four months and then comes the harvest? behold, I say unto you. Lift up your eyes, and look on the fields; for they are white already to harvest...both he that soweth and he that reapeth may rejoice together"* (John 4:34-35).

While we all may not be called to be evangelists, we are *all* called to find time to do evangelism work—to sow the Word of God in men's hearts, to prepare them for the coming of the Evangelist.

CONCLUSION

The purpose of the Body of Christ is to produce and further develop disciples for the sake of presenting an undeniable witness for Christ in the world. Evangelism is the starting point and indispensable catalyst in disciple making. Evangelism is not a "special" activity to be undertaken at a prescribed time, by a particular segment of the fellowship, but should be a constant and spontaneous outflow of ones individual and corporate experience of Christ. A disciple is a believer striving to be more like Christ by obediently growing in character and ability, in order to minister to others and produce more disciples.

Soul-winning is the responsibility of every ministry in the Church, and in order for a church to have effective discipleship, every church member needs to be committed to grow as a disciple, to be trained to use his or her gifts to edify the Body. Empowered by the Holy Spirit, they will be able to minister to new converts. It should never be assumed that everyone has been nurtured, and therefore understands in detail, all of the Christian essentials i.e., Salvation, prayer, ordinances of the church, temptation, the work of a Christian, stewardship and the grace of giving, etc. A thorough effort to teach or reinforce certain aids to Christian living should be a part of an evangelistic ministry.

My prayer is that a spiritual awakening will come to the Body of Christ, igniting among the people an insatiable thirst for God, a passion to seek the lost, and a *tongue of fire* that will lift Jesus Christ, higher than He's ever been lifted before!

NOTES

1. Leroy Eims (1978), *The Lost Art of Disciple Making,* Grand Rapids, Michigan: Zondervan Publishing House, p. 11.
2. Life Application Bible KJV (1989), Wheaton, Illinois: Tyndale Publishers, p. 1872.
3. Joseph C. Aldrich (1981), *Life-Style Evangelism,* Portland Oregon: Multnomah Press, p. 11.
4. Avert T. Willis, Jr., *Chronological Bible Storying,* Nashville, Tennessee: Broadman & Holman Publishers, p. 4.
5. Leonard Ravenhill, *John the Baptist and the Fire of God,* A Sermon, page 1.
6. Matthew Henry, *Commentary on the Whole Bible* (1961) Zondervan, p. 1525.
7. John R. Mott, *What Is Evangelism,* Vol. 3 of The Tambaram Series (London: Oxford University Press, 1939), pp. 48-62.
8. Commission on Evangelism (1943), *Towards the Conversion of England,* Westminster: The Press and Publications Board of the Church Assembly, p. 1.
9. D.T. Niles (1951), *That They May Have Life,* New York: Harper and Brothers Publishers, p. 96.

10. John Stott (1975), *The Lausanne Covenant,* Minneapolis: World Wide Publications, pp. 20-24.
11. Donald McGavran and Arn Winfield (1977), *Ten Steps for Church Growth,* New York: Harper and Row Publishers, p. 51.
12. George C. Hunter III (1979), *The Contagious Congregation,* Nashville: Abingdon, pp. 26, 28, 30-31.
13. Delos Miles (1983), *Introduction To Evangelism,* Nashville: Broadman & Holman Publishers, p. 47.
14. Ibid., p. 66.
15. Rick Warren (2002), *The Purpose-Driven Life,* Grand Rapids, Michigan, p. 282.
16. Ibid, p. 53.
17. Life Application Study Bible KJV, Tyndale Publishers, Luke 10:19.
18. Tony Evans (1999), *The Kingdom Agenda,* Nashville: World Publishing, p. 242.
19. Delos Miles, op. cit., p. 29.
20. Ibid., p. 29.
21. Ibid., p. 31.
22. Ibid., p. 25.
23. Herbert Lockyear (1996), *All The Men of the Bible/All the Women of the Bible,* Grand Rapids, Michigan, p. 49.
24. Rick Warren (1995), *The Purpose Driven Church,* Grand Rapids, Michigan, p. 77.
25. Walter Thomas Connor (1937), *Christian Doctrine,* Nashville, Tennessee, p. 22.
26. Tony Evans (1995), *Are Christians Destroying America?* Nashville, p. 85.
27. Leroy Eims, op. cit., p. 26.
28. Ibid., p. 181.
29. Ibid., p. 182.
30. Bill Bright (1993), *Witnessing Without Fear,* Nashville, Tennessee, p. 54.
31. "Zion Methodism: The State of the Country Committee"

(2001), *State of the Country Report*, p. 2.
32. Darrell W. Robinson (1995), *People Sharing Jesus*, Nashville, Tennessee, p. 133.
33. Walter A. Henrichsen (1998), *Disciples Are Made Not Born*, Colorado Springs, Co., p. 78.
34. Leroy Eims, op. cit., p. 62.
35. Walter Henrichsen, op. cit., p. 80.
36. J. E. O'Day (1985), op. cit., p. 5.
37. Ibid., p. 16.

BIBLIOGRAPHY

Aldrich, Joseph C. (1981), *Life-Style Evangelism,* Portland, Oregon: Multnomah Press.
Barna, George (2001), *Growing True Disciples,* Colorado Springs, Colorado: Waterbrook Press.
Bright, Bill (1993), *Witnessing Without Fear,* Nashville: Thomas Nelson, Inc.
Conner, William Thomas (1937), *Christian Doctrine,* Nashville: Broadman Press.
Eims, Leroy (1978), *The Lost Art of Disciple Making,* Grand Rapids, Michigan: Zondervan Publishing House.
Evans, Tony (1999), *The Kingdom Agenda,* Nashville: Word Publishing.
Henrichsen, Walter A. (1974), *Disciples Are Made Not Born,* Colorado Springs, Colorado: Chariot Victor Publishing.
Hull, Bill (1998), *Revival That Reforms,* Grand Rapids: Baker Book House.
Lockyer, Herbert (1996), *All The Men of the Bible,* Grand Rapids: Zondervan Publishing House.
Miles, Delos (1983), *Introduction to Evangelism,* Nashville: Broadman & Holman.

Pippert, Rebecca Manley (1979), *Out of the Saltshaker & into the World,* Downers Grove, Illinois: Intervarsity Press.
Reese, J. Irving (1989), *Simple Studies in Christian Essentials,* Elyria, Ohio: Baptist Mission of North America.
Robinson, Darrell W. (1995), *People Sharing Jesus,* Nashville: Thomas Nelson Publishers.
Warren, Rick (1995), *The Purpose-Driven Church,* Grand Rapids: Zondervan Publishing House.
Warren, Rick (2002) *The Purpose-Driven Life,* Grand Rapids: Zondervan Publishing House.

APPENDIX

NINE WORDS TO DESCRIBE EVANGELISM

1. **Martureo** - *Sharing* one's experience with others.
   Christians are to witness, for Jesus said, "You shall be my witnesses" (Acts 1:8). Witnesses *share* what they have seen and heard. This Greek verb, martureo is related to the English word "martyr," and implies both *being* and *bearing a witness.*
2. **Laleo** - *Talking* to others.
   A second Greek verb used to describe New Testament evangelism is laleo, which means to talk or use the voice. "As they spake to the people" (Acts 4:1) simply means they communicated a message. They were sharing the Gospel as they spoke to the people.
3. **Euaggelizo** - *Telling* others about Jesus.
   Evangelizing means to announce a Good News message. The New Testament Christians evangelized, or told others the Good News about Jesus. "Therefore they that were scattered abroad went everywhere preaching (evangelizing) the word" (Acts 8:4). A third Greek word used

to describe evangelism is euaggelizo, which means to gospelize, or to give the Gospel message. Much emphasis of this verb is on the message or matter announced.
4. **Didasko** - *Teaching* others the Gospel systematically.
A fourth kind of New Testament evangelism involves the systematic teaching of the Gospel. Jesus spoke of "teaching them to observe all things that I have commanded you" (Matt. 28:20). The Greek word didasko suggests a systematic explanation of the Gospel so that people can *understand and believe.*
5. **Dialegomai** - *Answering* reasonable objections.
A fifth Greek word, dialegomai means to reason or to respond to objections. When Paul and others in the New Testament engaged in evangelism, they often had to answer "reasonable objections" which were raised to the Gospel message. Paul's evangelism, at times, resembled a question and answer session. "And he reasoned in the Synagogue every Sabbath, and persuaded the Jews and Greeks" (Acts 18:4).
6. **Kataggello** - *Driving home* the Gospel.
A sixth Greek word used to describe evangelism is kataggello, which means the "driving home" of an idea. Effective evangelism reaches people at their point of need. When the unsaved realize how Jesus can meet that need in their lives, they can be led to conclude, "Jesus whom I preach unto you *is* Christ (Acts 17:3).
7. **Kerusso** - *Announcing* the Gospel so that people can respond.
The early Church proclaimed, or kerusso the Gospel so that people could understand and respond to it. They "preached Christ to them" (Acts 8:5). This Greek word is sometimes translated "heralding," or proclaiming as a herald.
8. **Mathateuo** - *Convincing* others to follow Jesus.
Jesus used the word mathateuo, or "make disciples" to

describe evangelism. "Go ye therefore, and make disciples" (Matthew 28:19 NIV), and it means to bring people to a conversion experience, to become lifelong followers of Christ. Jesus' use of this term may be the only use of the verb in the New Testament.

9. **Peitho** - *Persuading* those who are hesitant.
The biblical basis of evangelism as persuasion is found in the word "peitho," which means "to bring another to a point of decision." Paul stated, "knowing therefore, the terror of the Lord, we persuade men" (2 Corinthians 5:11). When he preached at Corinth, "he reasoned in the synagogue....and persuaded..." (Acts 18:4). This does not mean that Christians can talk others into being saved, but that they should attempt, like Paul, to fervently persuade others.

PROFILES: CONVERT, DISCIPLE, WORKER, AND LEADER

Profile of a Convert
    A. He or she gives evidences of possessing new life (2 Corinthians 5:17).
    B. His or her attitude toward Jesus Christ is now favorable, and the attitude toward sin is thus unfavorable.

Profile of a Growing Disciple
    A. As a follower of Jesus Christ, the growing disciple puts Him first in the major areas of his or her life, and is taking steps to separate from sin (Romans 12:1-2; Luke 9:23).
    B. The growing disciple continues in the Word through Bible Study and Scripture memory, and is consistent in applying the Word to his or her life, with the help of the Holy Spirit (Psalm 119:59; John 8:31; James 1:22-25).
    C. The disciple is growing in faith, and maintains a consistent devotional life. He or she is also committed to intercessory prayer (Hebrews 11:6; Colossians 4:2-4; Mark 1:35).
    D. Church attendance is regular, and the disciple demonstrates the love of Christ by fellowshiping with, and serving others (Psalm 122:1; John 13:34-35; Galatians 5:13; 1 John 4:20-21).

E. The growing disciple openly identifies with Christ where he or she lives, works, or socializes, and maintains a heart for witnessing—readily sharing his or her testimony as the opportunity arises (Matthew 5:16; Colossians 4:6; 1 Peter 3:15).
F. The growing disciple is a learner who is open as well as teachable (Acts 17:11).

Profile of a Worker

A. A *worker* evidences growth in all the virtues and skills outlined under the *Profile of a Growing Disciple* (1 Peter 3:18).
B. He or she shows a deep and growing compassion for the lost, and demonstrates an ability to lead people to Christ personally (Romans 1:6; Matthew 9:36-38).
C. He or she is consistently engaged in the art of making disciples.
D. Consistent study of the Word, and pursuit of the fruit of the Spirit are an integral part of his or her life (2 Timothy 2:15).

Profile of a Leader

A. A leader is an equipped worker who evidences growth in all the skills and virtues outlined under *Profile of a Worker.*
B. He or she is being used of God to help disciples to become workers (2 Timothy 2:2).
C. He or she shows capability of banding and leading workers in evangelism and spiritual growth (Mark 1:38).
D. Faithfulness and integrity are a part of his or her life and ministry (2 Timothy 2:19-21).

DISCIPLESHIP AND EFFECTIVE COMMUNICATION

Disciple by Example
    A. Jesus as a Role Model—He discipled His chosen twelve by example (John 13:15).
    B. Paul as a role model—he exhorted Timothy to lead by example in all things (1 Tim. 4:12).

Disciple by Life Application
    A. God expects us to teach people how to live. Sound doctrine is vital, but people also need to know how to deal with the practical issues of life.
    B. Over 3,000 sermons may be preached on Sunday, without anyone being saved; yet, on the day of Pentecost, that same number of souls were added to the Church.. Hence, our Gospel messages and sermons must be applicable to everyday life.
    C. We must teach people more about who they are in Christ, and less about what they need to do. They need to learn about peace, joy, and righteousness, which is what the Kingdom of God is all about (Romans 14:17).
    D. People must have peace with God, themselves, and other people, if they are ever going to enjoy their lives (Psalm 85:10; 1 Peter 3:10-11).
    E. Some people cannot have peace and joy because they

do not like themselves, and feel wrong, not right. They need help in finding peace in three realms: God, themselves, and other people.
    1. Peace with God is found in the doctrine of righteousness. We receive His righteousness at our *conversion* (2 Corinthians 5:21).
    2. Peace with yourself is found in self-acceptance and in believing you are righteous through Jesus Christ (Galatians 3:13).
    3. Peace with other people is found in treating them right—the "love walk."

F. When people are taught better, they *do* better.
    1. People need to know what types of things they should not watch on TV.
    2. People need to be reminded not to be selfish or self-serving.
    3. People need to be instructed not to abuse their credit cards, and how to handle their finances.
    4. Married people should be cautioned not to open the door for temptation.
        a. Riding to work with the opposite sex on a daily basis.
        b. Having lunch with the opposite sex.
        c. Appropriate dress.

Effective Communication

A. Be transparent; don't be afraid of offending/meddling.

B. Share your faults/weaknesses; struggles/victories.

C. Discuss moments of feeling defeat: times when you have been lonely; criticized; betrayed; judged; misunderstood, afraid, or perhaps, wanted to quit.

D. Be honest: tell them of times when you may have fallen asleep while praying.

E. Above all, do not try to impress people—HELP them!
F. Wounded healers must get help themselves.

Helping Hurting People
A. Ministers and other leaders must maintain balance in their own lives, in order to be able to help others:
1. We all need rest fun.
2. Everybody needs spiritual food, to avoid "burn-out."
3. We all need friends—including some who do not need something *from us*.

B. Teach people not to make excuses or blame others for their behavior, for God will ultimately take them back to that place.
C. Tell them that whatever they run from, or do not deal with will subsequently "deal" with them.

Printed in the United States
28839LVS00002B/61-108